A HISTORY OF EUROPE IN 12 CAFÉS

By the same author

Children Against Hitler: The Young Resistance Heroes of the Second World War

The Paper Bridge: A Return to Budapest

Deadly Carousel: A Diva's Exploits in Wartime Budapest

Long Lost: The Story of the Newspaper Column that Started the Reunion Industry

Raven: My Year of Dating Dangerously

For children

Benny and Bobby Versus Adolf: How Two Lab Mice Took on an Evil Empire

Dreams and Doorways: Turning Points in the Early Lives of Famous People

A HISTORY OF EUROPE IN 12 CAFÉS

MONICA PORTER

PEN & SWORD HISTORY
AN IMPRINT OF PEN & SWORD BOOKS LTD.
YORKSHIRE – PHILADELPHIA

First published in Great Britain in 2024 by
PEN AND SWORD HISTORY
An imprint of
Pen & Sword Books Ltd
Yorkshire – Philadelphia

ISBN 978 1 39903 152 3

A CIP catalogue record for this book is available from the British Library.

Typeset in Times New Roman 10.5/13 by
SJmagic DESIGN SERVICES, India.
Printed and bound in England by CPI Group (UK) Ltd.

Pen & Sword Books Ltd. incorporates the Imprints of Pen & Sword Archaeology, Atlas, Aviation, Battleground, Discovery, Family History, History, Maritime, Military, Naval, Politics, Railways, Select, Transport, True Crime, Fiction, Frontline Books, Leo Cooper, Praetorian Press, Seaforth Publishing, Wharncliffe, White Owl and After the Battle.

For a complete list of Pen & Sword titles please contact

PEN & SWORD BOOKS LIMITED
George House, Units 12 & 13, Beevor Street, Off Pontefract Road,
Barnsley, South Yorkshire, S71 1HN, United Kingdom
E-mail: enquiries@pen-and-sword.co.uk
Website: www.pen-and-sword.co.uk

or

PEN AND SWORD BOOKS
1950 Lawrence Rd, Havertown, PA 19083, USA
E-mail: uspen-and-sword@casematepublishers.com
Website: www.penandswordbooks.com

MIX
Paper | Supporting responsible forestry
FSC® C013604

In memory of my father, Péter Halász,
literary role model and café companion

‘Our finest place of education for everything new was the coffee house … an institution of a special kind which is not comparable to any other in the world. It is actually a kind of democratic club, accessible to anyone for an inexpensive cup of coffee.’

Stefan Zweig
From *The World of Yesterday*, 1942

Contents

List of Illustrations

Preface

Naturally, this book is not a comprehensive history of our great continent of Europe. Such a chronicle would require a library of books and more than one lifetime. What I offer instead is a waltz through six centuries, nine European countries (with America thrown in for good measure), and myriad episodes of history featuring some of the most intriguing and influential human beings who ever lived. And playing its vital role in all their stories, at times in the background, at times front and centre, is that exemplary breeding ground of ideas, the café.

INTRODUCTION

Perhaps it's not too fanciful to suggest that the café or coffee house and the hot black beverage consumed therein have been instrumental in forging the modern world. For centuries, this combination fuelled revolutions that upended regimes and these establishments hosted brainstorming sessions and intellectual debates that brought about new philosophies, advances in the sciences, and artistic and literary movements. They were a second home (and often more akin to a primary home) to the rebels, innovators and forward-thinkers of their age, across the political spectrum. They helped to create a lifestyle and what we think of as 'society'.

The café had a different kind of atmosphere to the tavern, the restaurant, the alehouse or pub; it had its own special allure. You could go to a café to be on your own – to meditate, write, create – and yet not be alone. Or you could go to join your circle of like-minded companions and sit for hours over cups of strong coffee that sharpened your wit and conversation, as opposed to congregating in a pub or bar, with your senses growing ever duller from alcohol.

My parents met at the Japan Coffee House in Budapest, soon after the Second World War. It was an elegant nineteenth-century establishment, well known for its literary and artistic clientele. My father was a writer, my mother a singer and actress, and they both had an appointment there with a mutual friend, a theatre director. He introduced them to each other; six months later, they were married.

So I was born out of an encounter in a café. Has that left its mark in my blood, perhaps? All I know is that I've always been drawn to café life, to its pleasures and consolations, its fascinating associations with the past. As a 19-year-old fledgling writer on my first visit to Paris in the 1970s, I sat down in one of the famous old Left Bank cafés where, a half-century earlier, the likes of Hemingway and Fitzgerald once sat, musing and penning their immortal lines over cups of *café noir*. Naturally, I followed suit, ruminating and scribbling into my notebook while sipping a *café au lait*. (As I well knew, the Right Bank was for the bourgeois life, the Left Bank for *la vie bohème*.) When I looked up, I noticed a group of young people at the next table eying me with amusement, smirking and sniggering at the little tourist who evidently regarded herself as some kind of latter-day Simone de Beauvoir, or maybe Françoise Sagan. But I didn't let it bother me, much.

Back home in London I loved to sit by the window of an Italian café near our home in Bayswater, jotting down notes for stories, people-watching, listening to the hum of conversation and the hissing steam of the espresso machine. It seemed that during such solitary meditations in a comfortable café – detached from the whirlwind of the city streets, yet able to observe them – thoughts and ideas would enter your mind that might not have done otherwise. There was a sort of alchemy at play.

Europe is now in its fifth century of coffee drinking and café-going. It's undeniable that the technological and cultural changes of the past few decades have greatly altered the role of both the beverage and the venue designed for its consumption. A coffee in a takeaway cup is what you might stop to pick up on your way to somewhere else. And if you do hole up for an hour or two, in a Starbucks, a Costa Coffee or a Nero, it's probably to use the Wi-Fi on your laptop and phone, with little attention to the others around you. Sadly, we nowadays mostly prefer to live in our own screen-dominated worlds. And yet, so much of what was conceived and forged in past epochs by the habitués of Europe's legendary cafés continues to influence our lives today. Our views on political and social issues, our perspectives on art and literature, our attachment to the tenets of humanism – indeed, our very Age of Enlightenment – were arguably born out of heated debates in the cafés of the great cities of Europe.

The miracle is how so many of these storied establishments are still in existence, despite the devastation wreaked by two world wars, foreign occupations, plenty of revolutions, the Great Depression and two global pandemics. A few of the cafés featured in this book almost didn't make it, being nearly felled for good either by a catastrophic loss of business during the Covid-19 lockdowns and travel bans of 2020 and 2021, or due to massive increases in rent demanded by rapacious landlords.

It may be true that in our present times these cherished historic cafés are more frequented by tourists than by 'movers and shakers' who gather in them to develop ideas that will transform the world. And by and large, they are a lot pricier than they were in the past, when even the most impecunious poet or artist could sit there hour after hour, for a pittance, reading the newspapers, conversing with friends, keeping warm.

But despite this, cafés still offer some of the most romantic and theatrical backdrops to life's dramas. This is clear from the many film scenes set in them. For example, Budapest's opulent nineteenth-century New York Café has appeared in several Hollywood movies, including the 2012 *Bel Ami*, starring Uma Thurman and Kristin Scott Thomas, when it doubled as a Parisian café of the Belle Époque, and the 2018 spy film *Red Sparrow*, starring Jennifer Lawrence and Jeremy Irons, in which it was a lavish restaurant in contemporary Moscow. The Caffè Florian in St Mark's Square, Venice, dating from 1720, was the setting for a scene in the 1999 film *The Talented Mr Ripley*, with Gwyneth Paltrow, Jude Law and Matt Damon, as well as one in 2014's *Effie Gray*, starring Dakota Fanning and Emma Thompson. Some scenes in the recent ITV psychological thriller series *Vienna Blood*, set in the Austrian capital in the early 1900s, were shot in the Café Sperl, whose handsome exterior and well-preserved, stylish interior have hardly changed since that era (even the billiard tables are still in situ). The Sperl also featured earlier, in the 1995 romantic film *Before Sunrise*, starring Julie Delpy and Ethan Hawke, and David Cronenberg's 2011 historical drama *A Dangerous Method*, about Sigmund Freud and Carl Jung.

The world moves on, the old allure of the historic cafés remains.

Chapter One

THE DISCOVERY OF COFFEE

In the year AD 850 or thereabouts, so the legend goes, a young goat herder in Ethiopia by the name of Kaldi observed something peculiar. Whenever his goats munched on the red berries of a particular type of bush native to the area, they became friskier, leaping about the hills with greater energy. Kaldi decided to try these berries himself and found they had the same effect on him. This curious phenomenon came to the attention of a local Muslim holy man, who also consumed a few of the berries and discovered to his delight that they allowed him to stay up all night, praying. And so, thanks to the humble goat, the extraordinary properties of the flowering plant known as *coffea arabica* made themselves known to humans.

Before long, consumption of coffee beans – the twin pips inside the coffee berry – was enthusiastically embraced by the followers of Sufism, the mystic strand

Kaldi and his goats discover the power of coffee in the hills of Ethiopia, *c.* AD 850.

of Islam. The Sufis worked during the day and practised their devotions at night. They were the renowned whirling dervishes, and anyone who has witnessed this whirling will agree that it takes a lot of energy to keep doing it all night. A stimulant would have been most handy.

To begin with, the coffee berries were either boiled whole, including the red husk, and the liquid drunk, or were ground up and mixed with oil or animal fat to create a paste, and eaten as a snack. From Ethiopia, coffee consumption made the short leap across the Red Sea to Yemen and it was there, over the following centuries, that the cultivation of *coffea arabica* began in earnest. From the fourteenth century, they started exporting the beans from their Red Sea port of Mocha, which became so closely associated with the trade that it gave its name to the commodity.

During the fifteenth century, Arab merchants and traders brought coffee from the Arabian Peninsula to the lands of the Eastern Mediterranean – the Levant – and into the Ottoman Empire. And the Ottoman Turks took to it with a greater fervour than anyone, as a social drink. The Arabs called it *qahwah*, an abbreviation of *qahhwat al-bun*, 'wine of the bean'. From this came the Turkish word *kahve*. When the Turks introduced coffee drinking to their recently conquered capital Constantinople, the result was the opening of the world's first designated coffee house, Kiva Han, in 1475. Soon there was a growing number of coffee houses – the Turks called them *kahveh kanes* – and they were frequented by all the classes. Everyone appreciated the opportunity they gave for social intercourse (men only) and open discussion. As they grew in popularity they became ever more luxurious, with richly furnished and carpeted lounges, and in addition to coffee, they often provided musical and other entertainments. The sultans were equally enthusiastic coffee drinkers at Topkapi Palace, where the coffee was prepared by specialist officials, the *kahvedjibachi*

Perhaps it was inevitable that at some point Ottoman religious leaders would rail against the coffee habit. A century after Kiva Han opened, the imams, preachers, and even the dervishes were complaining that while the coffee houses were full, the mosques were half empty. They declared that going to a coffee house was an even greater sin than entering a tavern: as Mohammed hadn't known about coffee and so couldn't have consumed it, it was an abomination for his followers to do so. The Grand Mufti ruled in favour of the diehard religious leaders and coffee was duly forbidden by law. But coffee drinking carried on in secret at Ottoman 'speakeasies', and was sold on the sly in the back rooms of shops. Bureaucrats were bribed to turn a blind eye. Eventually, a less rigorous Mufti came along who happened to enjoy coffee himself, and the prohibition was lifted … for a while.

Sultan Murad IV, who came to power in 1623 aged 11, once again banned coffee, along with tobacco and alcohol, and was particularly brutal in the punishments he decreed for those caught partaking of them. For a first violation the offender received a cudgelling, for a second (in emulation of ancient Rome) he was sewn up inside in a leather sack and thrown into the Bosporus. Murad IV – who in his more benign moods wrote poetry – had fifteen sons and thirteen daughters and died of liver cirrhosis at the age of only 27, which is unusual for a teetotaller. His early death was a boon to the empire's coffee aficionados: it was followed by a raging comeback for the cherished beverage.

The seventeenth-century French orientalist Antoine Galland related that during his lengthy sojourn in Constantinople in the 1670s there was no house, rich or poor, Turkish or Jewish, Greek or Armenian, where coffee was not drunk at least twice a day. It was also the custom in every house to offer it to visitors, it being considered rude not to. 'As much money must be spent by the families of Constantinople on coffee as on wine in Paris,' observed Galland, who also stated that whilst European beggars asked for money to buy wine or beer, it was for money to buy coffee that those of Constantinople held out their palms. What's more, it has been claimed that during that period of Ottoman history, refusing to provide one's wife with coffee was a legitimate cause for divorce. If true, what an astonishing turnabout from being drowned in the Bosporus inside a sack.

The established East-West trade routes inevitably carried coffee into continental Europe, though its progress was slow and for a while, it was a niche product, not for general consumption. It initially reached the great trading port of Venice in 1570, when the Italian botanist and physician Prospero Alpino brought bags of coffee beans back from his lengthy sojourn in Egypt. He regarded it as a medicinal drink and

An Ottoman coffee house in Constantinople, 1854 painting by Amadeo Preziosi.

Ripening coffee berries.

accordingly, it was sold in pharmacies, at great expense, to the wealthy. It was said to cure gout, wind, gallstones … pretty much any ailment. They made the brew by grinding the beans into a powder, which was then boiled and served with the grounds left in, making it dense and gritty – an earlier version of the Turkish coffee we know today. Very bitter, it remained so until its consumers realised they could just add sugar, and eventually, milk.

Within little more than half a century, the general appeal of this exotic, aromatic beverage from the East would, with the arrival of our first coffee houses, sweep through the metropolises of Europe. And so was born the European public's love affair with the coffee bean and all that became associated with it.

The dominance of the Arabs and Turks in the coffee trade diminished as the European powers began large-scale cultivation in their own colonies – the French created coffee plantations in the Caribbean islands of Martinique and Saint-Domingue (modern-day Haiti), the Dutch in Ceylon and Java, the Portuguese in Brazil.

Coffee is now grown in more than seventy countries, though the world's top five coffee producers are Brazil, Vietnam, Colombia, Indonesia … and Ethiopia, the land where it was fortuitously stumbled upon twelve centuries ago by Kaldi and his goats. Whilst coffee once entered Europe via Venice, today it is largely through Trieste, Italy's flourishing freeport on the other side of the Adriatic. Millions of bags of coffee beans arrive at the docks of Trieste each year from around the world, and are roasted and blended by the city's many roasteries – as you drive past them the strong scent of coffee can be exhilarating. The city has a number of lovely, historic cafés – one of the best being the Art Nouveau Caffè San Marco, dating back to 1914. And there is an annual coffee festival, with tastings, competitions and parties, and educational workshops at which children learn about Kaldi and 'the adventurous story of the coffee bean'.

Chapter Two

THE INVENTION OF THE EUROPEAN COFFEE HOUSE

The coffee house era in continental Europe began in 1647, with the opening of the first such establishment in St Mark's Square, Venice; unfortunately, little is known about it. The oldest existing picture of a coffee house in Europe was an etching by the Dutch artist Adriaen van Ostade, a pupil of Frans Hals. He specialised in showing the everyday lives of ordinary men and women, and in his *Dutch Coffee House* from 1650, coffee is being served to men sitting on low wooden chairs in a basic, unadorned room. The place still bore the characteristics of the tavern.

Holland has a long history in the coffee trade. It goes back to 1616, when Pieter van den Broecke, a merchant and administrator in the Dutch East India Company, stole some coffee plants from plantations in Mocha and took them back to Amsterdam – though regular imports of coffee from Mocha to Amsterdam didn't start until a half-century later. Eager to cultivate the crop themselves, the Dutch began doing so first in Ceylon (now Sri Lanka), and then, at the end of the seventeenth century – with great success – on the island of Java.

The Dutch readily adopted coffee consumption and the coffee house. But it would be safe to say that after the Turks, it was the English who became their greatest early champions. Some of us are now familiar with the story of Pasqua Rosée, who established London's first coffee house in St Michael's Alley, off Cornhill, in the bustling heart of the seventeenth-century capital. Rosée was an ethnic Greek Christian who had been living in the Ottoman port city of Smyrna as the servant of Daniel Edwards, an English merchant working for the Levant Company. (The company had been granted a charter by Queen Elizabeth I, who was eager to maintain trade, as well as a political alliance, with the Ottomans.) When Edwards returned to London in late 1651 – possibly because of an outbreak of the plague that autumn in Smyrna – he brought Rosée with him.

Edwards had developed a taste for coffee while living amongst the Turks, and continued to import it. He reputedly drank two or three 'dishes' of it at a time (before the invention of the coffee cup it was consumed from small and shallow, handleless bowls), and he did this at least twice a day. The coffee was prepared for him by his

The oldest known illustration of a European coffee house, 1650, by Adriaen van Ostade.

dutiful Greek servant, Rosée. Edwards' friends and associates would call on him daily to discuss business matters and to socialise, and they too enthusiastically imbibed the black brew. In the end, being fed up with these constant caffeinated intrusions, in 1652 Edwards set Rosée up with a little venue of his own where he could make and sell coffee publicly. At first, it was merely a kind of shed or stall, but very well sited in St Michael's Alley, within the medieval network of courts and alleyways opposite the Royal Exchange. It was an area teeming with merchants and traders.

Every morning they would gather at Rosée's shed to buy their dish of the brew, encouraged by the imaginative handbill he produced to advertise his product. It was headed 'The Vertue of the COFFEE Drink' and began: 'The Grain or Berry called Coffee, groweth upon little Trees, only in the Deserts of Arabia.' He described how the beans were turned into the drink, then listed the ailments it could remedy, including 'Dropsy, Scurvy, Hypocondriack Winds, Consumption and the Cough of the Lungs'. It could also 'prevent Mis-carryings in Child-bearing Women, and cure Children that have any running humors upon them, as the Kings Evil &c.' He explained that it prevented drowsiness, thereby making one 'fit for business'. But you shouldn't take it after supper, 'unless you intend to be watchful, for it will hinder sleep for 3 or 4 hours'. It was an early example of effective marketing.

Within a couple of years Rosée had made sufficient money to move into proper premises in St Michael's Alley, and it was this venue that has gained everlasting fame as London's first coffee house, 'At the Sign of Pasqua Rosée's Head'.

The timing couldn't have been better. Charles I had recently been beheaded and the country was ruled by Oliver Cromwell, the Lord Protector. As he and his Puritan followers abjured alcohol, linking it with sinful behaviour, the respectable new non-alcoholic beverage – promoted as a healthy alternative to beer and wine – received the republican government's wholehearted support. (Business at local taverns and alehouses suffered accordingly.)

Soon coffee houses were cropping up all over London. Within a decade, they numbered eighty-three and by the early eighteenth century, there were at least 550. Every man had his favourite coffee house. And by now it had become a way of life. (Of course, caffeine's addictive nature might have had something to do with this.) Sceptical contemporaries described coffee as tasting like 'puddle water', 'boiled shoes', 'syrup of soot', or worst of all, the drink that 'witches tipple out of dead men's skulls'. But that didn't stop most people from gulping it down. They liked that it energised them, mind and body, just as it had the whirling dervishes.

In his *History of England*, the Victorian writer Thomas Babington Macaulay wrote of this period:

> Foreigners remarked that it was the coffee house which specially distinguished London from all other cities; that the coffee house was the Londoner's home, and that those who wished to find a gentleman commonly asked, not whether he lived in Fleet Street or Chancery Lane, but whether he frequented the Grecian or the Rainbow.

Different coffee houses quickly became associated with different occupations, each developing its own clientele, its 'regulars'. There were coffee houses for lawyers, for

The Vertue of the *COFFEE* Drink.

First publiquely made and ſold in England, by *Paſqua Roſee.*

THE Grain or Berry called *Coffee*, groweth upon little Trees, only in the *Deſerts of Arabia.*

It is brought from thence, and drunk generally throughout all the Grand Seigniors Dominions.

It is a ſimple innocent thing, compoſed into a Drink, by being dryed in an Oven, and ground to Powder, and boiled up with Spring water, and about half a pint of it to be drunk, faſting an hour before, and not Eating an hour after, and to be taken as hot as poſsibly can be endured; the which will never fetch the skin off the mouth, or raiſe any Bliſters, by re ſon of that Heat.

The Turks drink at meals and other times, is uſually *Water*, and their Dyet conſiſts much of *Fruit*, the *Crudities* whereof are very much corrected by this Drink.

The quality of this Drink is cold and Dry; and though it be a Dryer, yet it neither *heats*, nor *inflames* more then *hot Poſſet.*

It encloſeth the Orifice of the Stomack, and fortifies the heat within it's very good to help digeſtion; and therefore of great uſe to be bout 3 or 4 a Clock afternoon, as well as in the morning.

uen quickens the *Spirits*, and makes the Heart *Lightſome.*

Is good againſt ſore Eys, and the better if you hold your Head o'er it, and take in the Steem that way.

It ſuppreſſeth Fumes exceedingly, and therefore good againſt the *Head-ach*, and will very much ſtop any *Defluxion of Rheums*, that diſtil from the *Head* upon the Stomack, and ſo prevent and help *Conſumptions*; and the *Cough of the Lungs.*

It is excellent to prevent and cure the *Dropſy, Gout*, and *Scurvy.*

It is known by experience to be better then any other Drying Drink for *People in years*, or *Children* that have any *running humors* upon them, as *the Kings Evil.* &c.

It is very good to prevent *Miſ-carryings in Child-bearing Women.*

It is a moſt excellent Remedy againſt the *Spleen*, *Hypocondriack Winds*, or the like.

It will prevent *Drowſineſs*, and make one fit for buſines, if one have occaſion to *Watch*; and therefore you are not to Drink of it *after Supper*, unleſs you intend to be *watchful*, for it will hinder ſleep for 3 or 4 hours.

It is obſerved that in Turkey, where this is generally drunk, that they are not trobled with the Stone, Gout, Dropſie, or Scurvey, and that their Skins are exceeding cleer and white.

It is neither *Laxative* nor *Reſtringent.*

Made and Sold in St. *Michaels Alley* in *Cornhill*, by *Paſqua Roſee*, at the Signe of his own Head.

Handbill advertising Pasqua Rosée's original 'coffee shed' in St Michael's Alley, London, 1652.

merchants, for printers, stock traders, insurers, money changers, auctioneers, some for clergymen and some for military men, still others for scholars from nearby Gresham College. There was great commercial value in mingling with other people from your trade or profession. It was the best way of exchanging ideas, staying on top of the news and the gossip, and hearing about developments affecting your line of work.

Lloyd's Coffee House, where shipping merchants met, morphed into Lloyd's of London, the insurance company. Christie's and Sotheby's were both born out of coffee houses that doubled as auction salerooms. The London Stock Exchange had its beginnings in Jonathan's Coffee House, where brokers met to set stock and commodity prices. Certain coffee houses near Parliament were patronised by politicians – some by Tories, others by Whigs. The satirist Jonathan Swift mocked the 'senators who are silent in the House, and loud in the Coffee-house, where they nightly adjourn to chew the cud of politics'.

At the Grecian Coffee House, off Fleet Street, scientists of the Royal Society met regularly. On one memorable occasion, Sir Isaac Newton and astronomer Edmond Halley (of comet fame) cleared a table of coffee cups so they could dissect a dolphin on it.

And then there was Will's Coffee House, a little further west in Covent Garden. This was the home of the 'Wits', whose leading light was poet and playwright John Dryden. The men there had no particular profession but were scribes of one sort or another, critics or satirists – reputedly sharp-witted to a man. It was a favoured haunt of Samuel Pepys, who praised it in his diary as a place of 'very witty and pleasant discourse'.

Such a staple of daily life in seventeenth-century London had these establishments become that in 1667 a play was put on called *The Coffee House*, by the playwright Thomas St Serfe. As a coffee house aficionado, Pepys naturally went to see it, together with his wife Elisabeth and their pretty young maid, Deb Willett. Pepys was not impressed, afterwards writing in his diary that it was 'the most ridiculous and insipid play I ever saw in my life'. Perhaps he was merely irritated because, even before the play began, Elisabeth complained about Deb 'sitting cheek by jowl' with them. Pepys believed his wife was jealous and resented his 'kindness' to the girl – and she had good reason to, as the notorious womaniser went on to seduce the comely Deb.

The long communal tables that were commonplace in coffee houses encouraged sociability; you were expected to speak to those seated next to you whether you knew them or not – a tradition maintained by the members-only gentlemen's clubs such as the Reform and the Garrick, which eventually emerged from the coffee house culture. Needless to say, the patrons seated at those tables were all men. The only women to be found in the coffee houses were there to serve the coffee, or in some cases were themselves the proprietor – an occupation considered respectable enough for a female. (One such was the Widow Smith, who ran the Turk's Head in the Strand.) But women didn't take part in the conversations, which revolved

A seventeenth-century London coffee house.

around male-orientated subjects such as politics, business and cultural criticism – not supposed to concern the 'fair sex'. Indeed, a major attraction of the coffee house for men was its distinction as their own domain, a place for them to associate with each other, without the distracting presence of women.

Those excluded females didn't necessarily accept the status quo without complaint. In 1674, they published *The Women's Petition Against Coffee* to protest against men's over-indulgence in the drink, arguing that the 'enfeebling liquor' made them impotent and therefore contributed to a falling birth rate. According to the petition, coffee made men 'as unfruitful as the sandy deserts, from where that unhappy berry is said to be brought'. What's more, they claimed the long hours that husbands spent in coffee houses kept them away from their domestic duties at home, and turned them into worse gossips than the women: 'they would soon learn to exceed us in Talkativeness: a Quality wherein our Sex has ever Claimed preheminence.'

But the women's protests were to no avail. That same year, a counter-pamphlet appeared: *The Men's Answer to the Women's Petition Against Coffee*, 'Vindicating their own Performances, and the Vertues of that Liquor, from the Undeserved Aspersions lately cast upon them'.

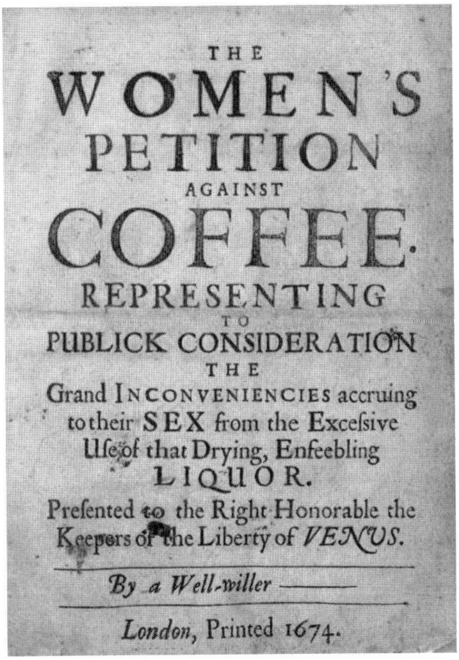

THE
WOMEN'S
PETITION
AGAINST
COFFEE.
REPRESENTING
TO
PUBLICK CONSIDERATION
THE
Grand INCONVENIENCIES accruing to their SEX from the Excefsive Ufe of that Drying, Enfeebling
LIQUOR.
Prefented to the Right Honorable the Keepers of the Liberty of *VENUS*.

By a Well-willer

London, Printed 1674.

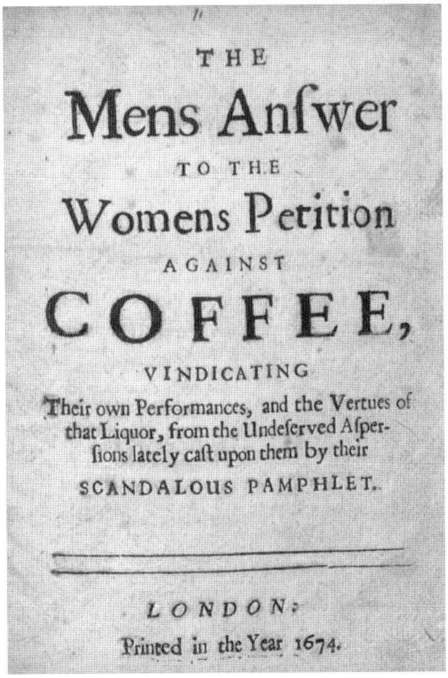

THE
Mens Anfwer
TO THE
Womens Petition
AGAINST
COFFEE,
VINDICATING
Their own Performances, and the Vertues of that Liquor, from the Undeferved Afperfions lately caft upon them by their
SCANDALOUS PAMPHLET.

LONDON:
Printed in the Year 1674.

***Above left*: The scathing *Women's Petition Against Coffee*, from 1674.**

***Above right*: And the rebuttal, *Men's Answer to the Women's Petition*.**

The activities at coffee houses could be downright dangerous. They gained a reputation during the Restoration period as hotbeds of dissent and intrigue, meeting places for freethinkers with ideas of anti-monarchism and religious insurrectionists. Macaulay refers to the 'Popish coffee-houses, where, as good Protestants believed, Jesuits planned over their cups another great fire, and cast silver bullets to shoot the King'.

Indeed, it was precisely for these reasons that in 1675 Charles II attempted to ban the places. His royal edict stated that they:

> have produced very evil and dangerous effects; as well for that many Tradesmen and others, do therein mis-spend much of their time … and by occasion of the meetings of such persons therein, diverse False, Malitious and Scandalous Reports are devised and spread abroad, to the Defamation of His Majesties Government, and to the Disturbance of the Peace and Quiet of the Realm.

The ban led to such a public outcry that within a fortnight the king had backtracked, the edict was withdrawn, and the coffee houses carried on happily. But their reputation for sedition remained. A rhyming couplet from a comic verse play of 1681 described the state of affairs:

> In a coffee house just now among the rabble
> I bluntly asked, which is the treason table?

Except for the fact that it was designed for men only, the coffee house was an exemplar of democracy. Any man could go in, pay a penny for his dish of coffee and benefit not only from worthwhile conversation but also from reading the many periodicals, pamphlets and news-sheets made freely available there. Coffee houses were thus dubbed 'penny universities'.

Not only did they circulate the news, they made it too. The writers Joseph Addison and Richard Steele founded *The Tatler* in 1709 and *The Spectator* in 1711 as publications aimed specifically at gathering news and gossip from the coffee houses, as well as reporting on their goings-on. (*The Spectator* is the world's oldest surviving weekly magazine – though its modern incarnation dates 'only' from 1828 – and to this day has a newsy blog called 'Coffee House'.)

Steele set the tone of *The Tatler* in its first issue with his announcement:

> All accounts of gallantry, pleasure and entertainment shall be under the article of White's Coffee House; poetry under that of Will's Coffee House; learning under the title of Grecian; foreign and domestic news you will have from St. James's Coffee House, and what else I shall on any other subject offer shall be dated from my own apartment.

And Addison did the same in the first number of *The Spectator*:

> There is no place of general resort wherein I do not often make my appearance. Sometimes I am seen thrusting my head into a round of politicians at Will's, and listening with great attention to the narratives that are made in those little circular audiences. Sometimes I smoke a pipe at Child's, and … overhear the conversation of every table in the room. I appear on Sunday nights at St. James's coffee house, and sometimes join the little committee of politics in the inner room as one who comes there to hear and improve. My face is likewise very well known at the Grecian [and] the Cocoa Tree … I have been taken for a merchant upon the Exchange for above these ten years, and sometimes pass for a Jew in the assembly of stock jobbers at Jonathan's; in short, wherever I see a cluster of people, I always mix with them.

In 1712, in Russell Street, Covent Garden, Addison established a coffee house for Daniel Button, a former servant in the Countess of Warwick's household. And a year later at Button's Coffee House, Addison and Steele launched a third newspaper, *The Guardian*, installing a white marble letterbox there in the form of a lion's head, 'with a most wide and voracious mouth' into which anyone could place written material for possible inclusion in the weekly paper. It carried a Latin inscription: *'Cervantur magnis isti cervicibus ungues: Non nisi delictâ pasciture ille ferâ,'* meaning, 'Those talons are kept for mighty necks: he feeds only on the beast of his choice.' In other words, Addison wanted his lion to be feared, but only by those who abused their power and wealth.

Addison responded to the public submissions with a weekly column, aptly called 'The Roaring of the Lion', and said he hoped 'to make him roar so loud as to be heard all over the British nation'. His lion, he declared, was 'a proper emblem of knowledge and action, being all head and paws'. The paper's contributors included Jonathan Swift and the poet Alexander Pope, and Button's served as its informal office. It was short-lived – from March to October 1713 – and no relation to *The Manchester Guardian* of a century later.

Perhaps the quirkiest coffee house, with the saddest outcome, was the brainchild of Richard Hogarth, father of artist William Hogarth. A classics scholar and writer of Latin and Greek textbooks for students, he was a passionate devotee of the Latin language. In need of money, in 1704 he hit upon the novel idea of opening a coffee house where only Latin could be spoken. He dedicated a room to it at his home, St John's Gate in Clerkenwell, and published an advertisement:

> There will meet daily some learned gentlemen, who speak Latin readily, where any Gentleman that is either skilled in that Language, or desirous to perfect himself in speaking thereof will be welcome. The Master of the House, in the absence of others, being always ready to entertain Gentlemen in the Latin Tongue.

The lion's head (designed by William Hogarth) at Button's Coffee House.

Alas, there were not enough ardent Latin speakers in London in the early eighteenth century to keep his business going, and after three years, it had to close. Now bankrupt, Hogarth was forced to spend five years in the Fleet debtors' prison, a grim place that his (far more successful) son would later depict in his series of paintings, *The Rake's Progress*.

But onward to the nineteenth century and it's all change. By the 1820s, our coffee houses were fast disappearing – England, importing vast quantities of tea

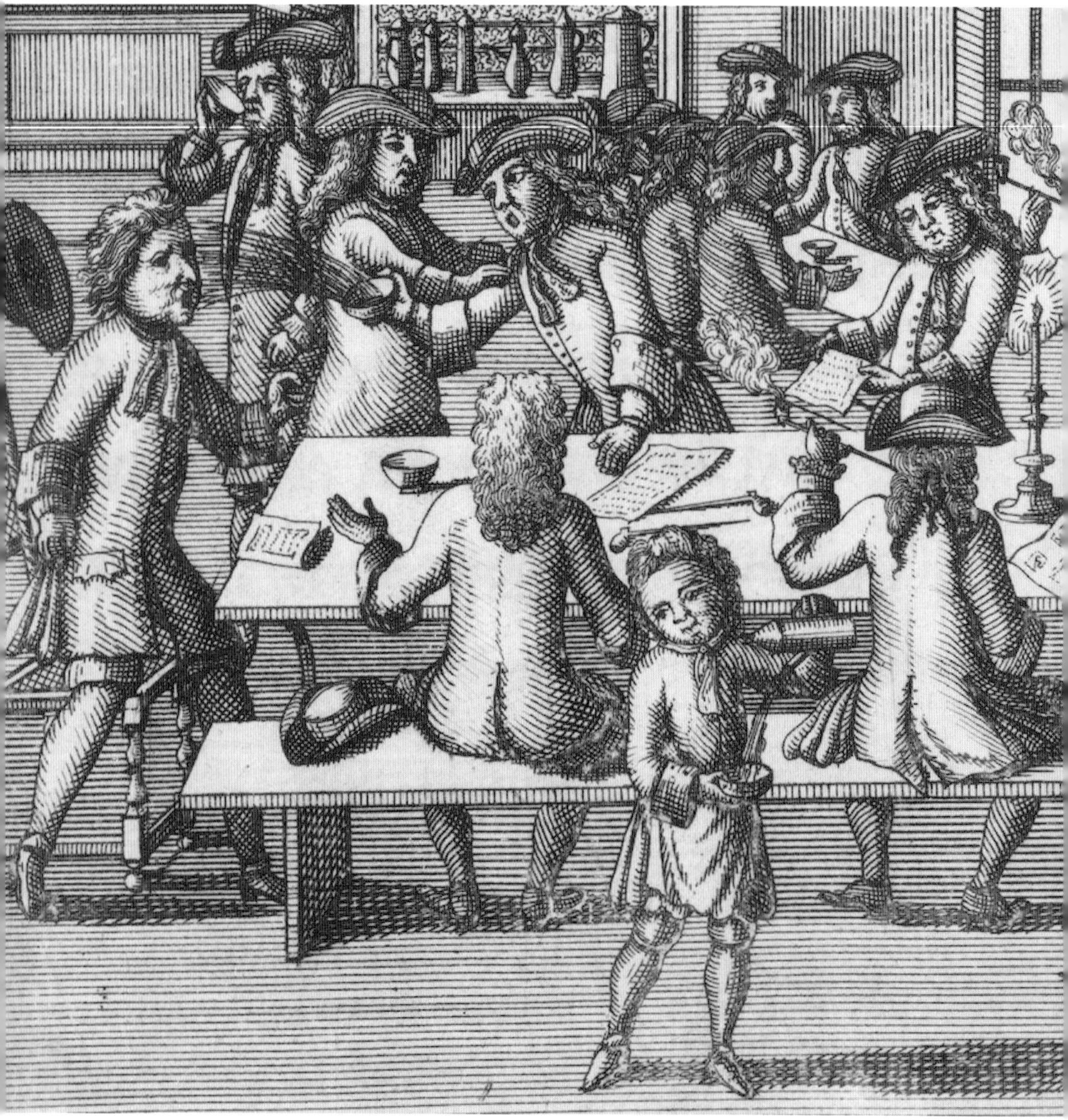

Tempers flare in an early eighteenth-century English coffee house.

from India, had turned into a tea-drinking nation. Coffee would not make a major comeback until the late twentieth century, with the advent of the international corporate chains. The notable exception was London's cosmopolitan, bohemian quarter of Soho, where the first Italian coffee bar, Bar Italia on Frith Street, was opened in 1949 by the Polledrini family. They continue to run it to this day. And four years later, Achille Gaggia's revolutionary espresso machine arrived in Soho as the centrepiece of the

***The Coffee-house Politicians*, English engraving, *c.*1733.**

The 2i's Coffee Bar, Soho, London, 1960s.

new Moka Coffee Bar, also on Frith street. A profusion of Italian-style espresso bars began springing up in Soho in the 1950s, all featuring a shiny new Gaggia machine, and instead of marble, the tabletops were made of Formica. They attracted a hip young crowd, stayed open late and as well as providing a jukebox, often featured live music from the budding young talents of the day. The 2i's Coffee Bar opened on Old Compton Street in 1956 and played a vital role in the emergence of rock 'n' roll music in Britain. Pop stars Tommy Steele, Cliff Richard and Adam Faith were all discovered there. The 'i's' referred to the two Iranian brothers, Freddie and Sammy Irani, who ran the establishment before it was taken over by a pair of professional wrestlers, Paul Lincoln and Ray Hunter.

Nowadays, the ubiquitous, identikit chain coffee outlets far outnumber traditional teashops on the streets of Britain. We buy lots of tea but it seems we mainly consume it at home whilst, as in bygone times, we like visiting a 'coffee shop' for our daily cappuccino, latte or macchiato. But could a branch of Starbucks ever be the birthplace of a cultural movement or trailblazing organisation, let alone an earth-shaking political revolution? It doesn't seem likely.

Then again, back in the 1990s, which isn't all that long ago, a poor aspiring author holed up in a café in Edinburgh to keep warm while penning her first book – in longhand, just like the literati of bygone times. And J.K. Rowling's efforts *did* go on to launch a revolution of sorts: the extraordinary Harry Potter industry, which transformed the children's literary landscape. So perhaps we should keep an open mind …

HERE STOOD
THE FIRST LONDON
COFFEE HOUSE
AT THE SIGN OF
PASQUA ROSEE'S HEAD
1652

CORPORATION OF LONDON
SITE OF
LLOYD'S
COFFEE HOUSE
1691-1785

THE CORPORATION OF
ON THIS SITE BETWEEN
1680 AND 1778 STOOD
JONATHAN'S COFFEE HOUSE,
THE PRINCIPAL MEETING
PLACE OF THE CITY'S
STOCKBROKERS

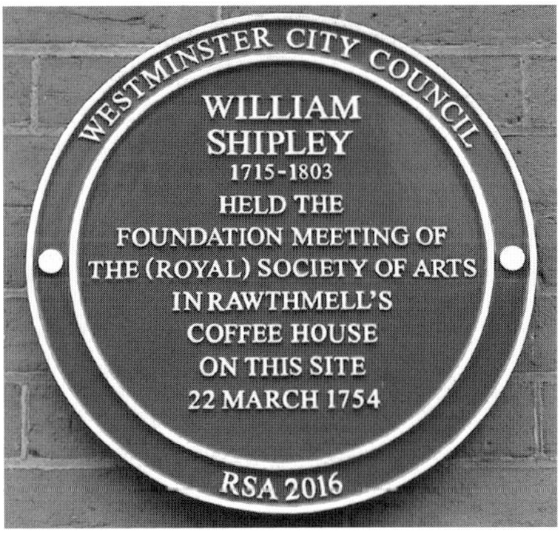
WESTMINSTER CITY COUNCIL
WILLIAM
SHIPLEY
1715-1803
HELD THE
FOUNDATION MEETING OF
THE (ROYAL) SOCIETY OF ARTS
IN RAWTHMELL'S
COFFEE HOUSE
ON THIS SITE
22 MARCH 1754
RSA 2016

CITY OF WESTMINSTER
SITE OF
OLD SLAUGHTERS
COFFEE HOUSE
WHERE ON
16th JUNE 1824
WAS FORMED THE SOCIETY
NOW KNOWN AS
RSPCA
ROYAL SOCIETY FOR THE PREVENTION OF CRUELTY TO ANIMALS

CITY OF WESTMINSTER
SITE OF THE
2i's COFFEE BAR
(1956-1970)
BIRTHPLACE OF
BRITISH ROCK 'N ROLL
AND THE POPULAR
MUSIC INDUSTRY
ROBERT MANDRY

Chapter Three

QUEEN'S LANE COFFEE HOUSE, OXFORD

Not one of London's celebrated coffee houses from the seventeenth and eighteenth centuries has survived into the twenty-first. All we have to remind us of them is the occasional blue plaque on a wall. There is one to commemorate the site of Pasqua Rosée's coffee house in St Michael's Alley, now occupied by a nineteenth-century pub called the Jamaica Wine House. Another on Lombard Street marks the spot where Lloyd's Coffee House stood from 1691 to 1785 (these days, it's a Sainsbury's). Yet another, on Change Alley, shows us where Jonathan's, 'principal meeting place of the City's stockbrokers', stood from 1680 to 1778. Mere reminders.

But it's a different story in Oxford. Not only can the great university city lay claim to opening a coffee house *before* London did, but its original site on the High Street is a café even today. What's more, it is directly opposite another historic coffee house, of similar vintage, and that too still fulfils the same function. True, the pair haven't been in continuous operation as coffee houses; for long periods they were home to other types of businesses. But in view of their historic significance, perhaps we can overlook that.

Coffee arrived early in Oxford because of the international draw of its famous university. The seventeenth-century diarist John Evelyn noted, with regard to the year 1637, when he began to study at Balliol College: 'There came in my time to the college one Nathaniel Conopios, out of Greece. He was the first I ever saw drink coffee; which custom came not into England till thirteen years thereafter.' This Greek student at Balliol, a native of Crete, was the first person ever recorded as brewing coffee in England. The seventeenth-century Oxford antiquarian Anthony Wood also wrote about Conopios in his book *Athenae Oxonienses*:

> It was observed that while he continued in Balliol College he made the drink for his own use called Coffey, and usually drank it every morning, being the first, as the ancients of that House have informed me, that was ever drank in Oxon.

In 1650 – two years before Rosée launched his coffee 'shed' in London – a Jewish immigrant from the Levant (some say Syria, others Lebanon), known only as

Jacob, opened England's first coffee house. This was the Angel, on the south side of Oxford High Street, 'and there it was by some, who delighted in noveltie, drank,' wrote Anthony Wood. Since 1997, the occupant of this site has been The Grand Café. Wood also recorded the arrival of Oxford's second coffee house in 1654, founded by another Levantine Jew, called Cirques Jobson. This stood on the north side of the High Street, at the corner of Queen's Lane (so called because it borders Queen's College), and is the present Queen's Lane Coffee House.

Coffee rapidly became a favourite beverage amongst the students of Oxford University. Their demand for it was such that in 1655 they urged an apothecary called Arthur Tillyard to prepare and sell 'coffey publickly in his house against All Soulcs College'. Tillyard's coffee house soon became the meeting place for a group calling itself the Oxford Chemical Club, composed of Oxford's leading scientists – most notably the pioneering chemist Sir Robert Boyle – and their students. They would gather there to share ideas and discuss their scientific theories and research, caffeine and intellectual zeal proving a winning combination. One keen attendee was Christopher Wren, then a fellow of All Souls and actively engaged in his own research. Only five years later this burgeoning scientific 'club' had relocated to London and evolved into the Royal Society, now the oldest and most famous scientific society in the world.

There is no longer any trace of the obliging Mr Tillyard's coffee house at All Souls; it didn't have the longevity of other Oxford coffee houses. The university authorities kept a close eye on these caffeine-fuelled dens of unsupervised discourse, especially those frequented by the more errant students. As in London, the political pamphlets, scandal sheets and radical publications of the day were read freely there, and this could lead to all sorts of trouble. However, it seems the authorities' main problem, after some coffee houses had been granted licences to sell wine, was the noisy mayhem caused late at night by drunken students. Regulations were brought in to try to curb the disturbances, but they had limited success. Apparently, student behaviour was as difficult to govern then as it is now.

Returning to our two extant establishments, facing each other in friendly competition on the High Street, The Grand Café (formerly the Angel, Est. 1650), in its elegant Grade II listed building, is clear winner for being the first coffee house not only in Oxford but in the whole of England. It was set up in a room in the Angel coaching inn, the premises subsequently becoming a fashionable hotel. Then, in the mid-nineteenth century, the Cooper family of grocers and wine merchants took it over and it was where Frank Cooper's wife, Sarah, began selling her homemade marmalade. A big hit with the customers, it's the Original Oxford Marmalade we still prize today. Later still, it was a Co-op, an ironmonger's, a post office and a teddy bear shop – a high street building with a colourful past.

But the establishment with the more long-lasting historic significance is the one across the street. The Queen's Lane Coffee House, in existence since 1970, these days styles itself with the snappier name of the 'QL Coffee House'. It too is housed in a Grade II listed building with an eighteenth-century frontage. In the second half of the 1700s, it was a coffee house known as Harper's, where an idea was born that was to have an enduring influence on the global political landscape.

A happy discovery

The philosopher and social reformer Jeremy Bentham (1748–1832) was a London-born child prodigy who could speak Latin at the age of 3. When he was 12, he was sent to study at Queen's College, Oxford, there gaining his Master's degree seven years later.

Afterwards, Bentham continued to spend time occasionally in Oxford, and as a Queen's College alumnus, naturally frequented the coffee house across the lane. It was there that he stumbled upon a piece of writing titled *The First Principles of Government and the Nature of Political, Civil and Religious Liberty*, by the political theorist Joseph Priestley. This work inspired Bentham to found the philosophy of utilitarianism, based on the principle that the best course of action is one that brings about the greatest good for the greatest number of people. As Bentham recalled later in his life:

> Dr Priestley published his Essay on Government in 1768. He there introduced as the only reasonable and proper object of government, 'the greatest happiness of the greatest number' ... Somehow or other, shortly after its publication, a copy of this pamphlet found its way into the little circulating library belonging to a little coffee-house attached to Queen's College, Oxford. It was a corner house, having one front towards the High Street, another towards a narrow lane, which on that side skirts Queen's College ...

Bentham, the 'Father of Utilitarianism', set out his theories in a vast number of writings, a great deal of his work being still unpublished at the time of his death. A firm believer in equal education for all, he was associated with the foundation in 1826 of University College London, which acquired the majority of his manuscripts and has since 1959 been running the Bentham Project. This aims to produce a comprehensive edition of his collected works, and a team of volunteers are currently transcribing some 60,000 digitised manuscript pages (30 million words).

Bentham's principles, which aim for the betterment of society as a whole, have been adopted throughout the Western world and permeate many areas of modern life. The American financial information website Investopedia explains some of the ways utilitarianism affects our actions and decisions, both public and private:

1. It is the only moral framework that can justify military force or war.
2. It is the most common approach to business ethics because of how it accounts for costs and benefits. For example, a pharmaceutical company

The building that housed Bentham's little corner coffee house (and England's first), in a nineteenth-century photo by William Henry Fox Talbot.

will release a drug which has been approved, though it has known minor side effects, because the drug can help more people than will be bothered by the side effects.

3. A business not only needs to make a profit, but must also be socially responsible, so companies must put ethics on a par with profits. Consumers look for companies they can trust, and employees work better when there are ethics in place.

4. If you make morally correct decisions at work, everyone's happiness will increase. If you choose to do something morally wrong – even if legal – then everyone's happiness, including your own, will decrease.
5. Policymakers in Western democracies generally promote free markets, along with some government interference in the private lives of citizens in order to ensure safety and security. Where disadvantaged groups suffer negative consequences because of a utilitarian-based policy, most politicians try to find a remedy.

And so on. In short, an action is right if it tends to promote happiness and wrong if it tends to produce unhappiness. Simple. Jeremy Bentham would be gratified to know that nearly two centuries after his death, not only is he still talked about and studied, there are also numerous people in many countries endeavouring to put his theories into practice.

In Bentham's own era his greatest admirer and follower was the philosopher, economist and Liberal MP John Stuart Mill, who became a key advocate of utilitarianism. Mill's father, the Scottish historian and political theorist James Mill, had met Bentham in 1808 and the two men became friends and allies. They joined forces in a campaign to transform what was an archaic, semi-feudal England into a modern democracy. Decades later, John Stuart Mill published *Utilitarianism*, in which he explained the ethics of Bentham's philosophy and defended it against criticisms and misunderstandings. The book has been described as the nineteenth century's 'most influential philosophical articulation of a liberal humanistic morality'.

Shortly before his death, Bentham requested in his will that his body be preserved, fashioned into what he called an 'auto-icon' and made accessible to his 'personal friends and other disciples'. The task was carried out by his friend, surgeon Thomas Southwood Smith, who later donated the skeletal remains – clothed in Bentham's garments, sitting in his chair and holding his cane – to University College London. The startling relic can be seen today inside a glass case at UCL's Student Centre in Gordon Square. Only the head is not Bentham's own; it is made of wax. After the original was stolen in a prank by students from a rival college, it spent many years locked away in a box. Recently, it has been put on public display again, but the desiccated head with its glass eyes is not a pretty sight.

All of this goes to show that even the wisest and noblest of philosophers is capable of putting something profoundly weird in his will.

As already mentioned, the original seventeenth-century coffee house that stood on the corner now occupied by QL was opened by one Cirques Jobson, émigré from the Eastern Mediterranean. By an interesting quirk, its present owner comes from the same region. Aylin Muldur and her family came to the UK from Turkey in 1982, when she was 13, and her parents bought the business. Aylin and her brother worked there every day after school, on weekends and during holidays, so the café

Jeremy Bentham portrait by Henry William Pickersgill, 1829.

The present-day Queen's Lane Coffee House.

business is, as she says, 'in her blood'. The rest of the family having passed away, she now runs it on her own.

Aylin is proud of her coffee house's venerable past and its significant footnote in the history of political philosophy in England as well as other Western cultures. She can be equally chuffed about the key role her Turkish forebears played in popularising the potent black brew in the first place, thereby creating the need for the coffee house itself.

Chapter Four

CAFÉ PROCOPE, PARIS

In 1686, two European cities welcomed their first coffee houses: Vienna and Paris. No one now knows how long the one in Vienna lasted; perhaps not much longer than the seventeenth century (there will be more on this coffee house later). But, very happily, the Paris establishment, the Café Procope, is still in business. The late seventeenth century was an excellent moment for Parisians to launch into coffee house culture, as it coincided with the birth of the Age of Enlightenment, the movement in which France was to play such a prominent role. Over subsequent decades, and in the lead-up to the French Revolution, Enlightenment luminaries – the likes of Voltaire and Rousseau and from America, Benjamin Franklin and Thomas Jefferson – congregated and thrashed out their ideas for changing the world at the caffeine-powered hub of discourse that was the Procope.

Coffee drinking had become fashionable among the elites in Paris some years earlier with the arrival of Suleiman Aga, the Ottoman Empire's ambassador to the Sun King, Louis XIV. Suleiman brought with him sacks of coffee beans and the equipment needed to make and serve coffee, treating Parisian high society to the exotic custom. The essayist Isaac D'Israeli, father of British Prime Minister Benjamin Disraeli, described the scene in his book of historical anecdotes, *Curiosities of Literature*:

> On bended knee, the black slaves of the Ambassador, arrayed in the most gorgeous Oriental costumes, served the choicest Mocha coffee in tiny cups of egg-shell porcelain, hot, strong and fragrant, poured out in saucers of gold and silver, placed on embroidered silk doylies fringed with gold bullion, to the grand dames, who fluttered their fans with many grimaces, bending their piquant faces – be-rouged, be-powdered and be-patched – over the new and steaming beverage.

The king himself was so taken with coffee drinking that he grew his own coffee beans in the greenhouses at Versailles. He enjoyed handpicking, roasting and grinding the beans, and preparing his own coffee in the ever more common European manner of filtering it through a cloth bag, rather than consuming it with the grounds included, as in the Turkish style.

The general populace of Paris got their taste of the brew from licensed street vendors – the *limonadiers* – mostly newcomers from the East. One such was an Armenian by

A street coffee vender in Paris, late seventeenth century.

the name of Pascal, whose kiosk in the 1670s sold refreshments such as lemonade, barley water and sorbets, as well as coffee. When he relocated to London, he left his *loge de la limonade* to his apprentice, a Sicilian named Francesco Procopio dei Coltelli.

Realising that coffee was a big draw, a few years later the ambitious Procopio upgraded the enterprise by moving to premises in the rue des Fossés-Saint-Germain-des-Prés on the Left Bank, and opening the first venue actually to be called a *café*. At first, it was so dark that people compared it to a gloomy cave, so Procopio furnished it with chandeliers, large wall mirrors and marble-topped tables for his customers to sit at – the fundamental components of what became classic European café décor. He also Gallicised his name to François Procope, and thus was founded the café of the same name. Alongside the earlier refreshments, he added a few simple Italian dishes and dressed his waiters in Armenian attire.

Three years later in 1689, the Comédie-Française, the state theatre company created by the king's decree, opened its venue across the street. This proved a real boon to Procope's business, as the café became the hangout of actors, playwrights, dramatists, musicians, stage designers and critics. Other cafés began to pop up in Paris – by the 1720s, there were around 400 – though the Procope remained among the best known. By then, following on the heels of the theatrical crowd, intellectuals gathered there. And Enlightenment thinking was well underway.

Literary salon

The first major push into the Age of Reason came from England, with the bloodless Glorious Revolution of 1688. It overthrew the Catholic King James II, replacing him with his Protestant daughter Mary and her Dutch husband, William of Orange. A year later, William and Mary signed the Bill of Rights, creating a constitutional monarchy that gave Parliament power over monarchs and guaranteed the civil rights of ordinary citizens. Influential philosophers such as John Locke in England, Adam Smith and David Hume in Scotland, Immanuel Kant in Germany, Voltaire in France, and the Genevan Jean-Jacques Rousseau advocated societies based on freedom, rights ensured under the law and equal opportunity for all. These liberalising tenets went

The Café Procope in Paris, eighteenth-century hub of the Enlightenment. *(Courtesy of the Wellcome Library, London)*

down well with the French middle classes of the eighteenth century. Educated and open-minded, they believed no one should be born into privilege but that a person's position in society should be based on merit. *Liberté, égalité, fraternité*, in fact.

The Procope became a veritable literary salon, frequented by the leading writers, theorists and philosophers of the period. Voltaire, its most enthusiastic habitué, was a legendary coffee drinker who reputedly wrote his Enlightenment treatises on forty cups a day, which he liked to mix with chocolate. That amount of caffeine would kill most people but merely fired Voltaire's brain to formulate his seminal beliefs: that social progress could be achieved through reason, that no authority should be immune to challenge by the same, and that political and religious tolerance were paramount. (Voltaire was also a fan of another of the Procope's attractions, ice cream, and is said to have once remarked: 'Ice cream is so exquisite, it's a pity it isn't illegal.')

The Procope was also where two prominent Enlightenment figures, writer-philosopher Denis Diderot and mathematician Jean le Rond d'Alembert, got together and conceived their idea to produce the *Encyclopédie*, a comprehensive encyclopaedia published in France over two decades, starting in 1751. Translated into English with the subtitle *A Systematic Dictionary of the Sciences, Arts and Crafts*, it represented the ethics of the Enlightenment, Diderot hoping it would 'change the way people think'. The decades-long work aimed to gather all the available knowledge in the world, examine it critically and rationally, and use it for the social advancement of the general public. It was the first encyclopaedia to include contributions from numerous named contributors – an example of the democratisation of knowledge – and argued for the secularisation of learning away from the Jesuits, who had created Europe's first free public education system in the sixteenth century and still controlled the schools.

American friends

Benjamin Franklin, America's first diplomat, was sent to France in 1776 with a commission to win support (i.e. money) for its war of independence from Britain. He was hugely popular with the French aristocracy and intellectuals, who embraced him as the personification of New World Enlightenment. While in Paris, he often stopped in at the Café Procope to drink coffee with the literati and discuss the political situation not only in America, vis-à-vis George III, but also in France with Louis XVI. He undoubtedly inspired republican notions in the minds of others.

Patrons at the Procope reported that Franklin spent time there sitting alone, quill pen in hand, drafting the Treaty of Amity and Commerce. This contract, signed with France in February 1778, recognised the United States as an independent nation and promoted trade between the two countries. There was no doubting Franklin's skills in diplomacy and negotiation – in the end, France provided the money, troops, armaments and naval support so crucial to the fledgling country. French nobles, meanwhile, queued up to cross the Atlantic to join the fight for American independence. Amongst them was the wealthy young Marquis de Lafayette, who was to become a star officer of George Washington's Continental Army as well as Washington's close personal friend.

After nine years in France, Franklin returned home to Philadelphia. Thomas Jefferson, who replaced him, followed suit in making the Procope his frequent retreat. When Franklin died a few years later, France's revolutionary government mourned the 'great friend of republicanism'. His cherished café draped its walls, inside and out, in black cloth, and conducted a memorial service in front of Franklin's portrait.

As the 1780s wore on, anger grew over Louis XVI's disastrous mismanagement of the country, which was leading it to the verge of bankruptcy (financing America's war was a major contribution to that). Paris turned into a hotbed of revolutionary turmoil, with its cafés at the heart of it – by then the city had an estimated 800 of them. Known for their patrons' loose talk, they were 'nerve centres' for *bruits publics* – public noises or rumours – and a better source of information than the newspapers available at the time. The cafés provided a buzzing network through which news was spread to the public, and chief among them was the Procope.

Grounds for revolution

During the turbulent days of 1789, the leading revolutionaries, fiery characters such as Maximilien Robespierre, Georges Danton, Camille Desmoulins and Jean-Paul Marat, could be found at the tables of the Café Procope, drinking coffee or something stronger, and debating the burning questions of the hour, full of hatred for the despotic rule of Louis XVI. Robespierre, a prominent lawyer and politician, declared that 'the King must die, so that the country can live'. He was to prove rather too bloodthirsty, however, when he later instigated his own Reign of Terror …

As it turned out, the spark that finally lit the revolution came not from the Procope but from the Café de Foy. And there was a good reason for this. The Foy was in the unique precinct of the Palais-Royal, domain of the nobleman Louis Philippe II, Duke of Orléans. The duke was not only more moderate than his cousin, the king, but had a revolutionary outlook himself. His Palais-Royal home faced a huge rectangular garden, open to the public, bordered on three sides by six-storey apartment buildings with ground-floor colonnades. These created shopping arcades with stores selling all manner of luxury goods, bookshops, museums, restaurants and cafés. It was a fashionable marketplace and an area for socialising, frequented by all the classes – aristocracy, bourgeoisie and workers. Since the police could not easily enter the Palais-Royal, it became a refuge for the monarchy's opponents, a focus of resistance bang in the middle of Paris. The Duke of Orléans protected the people's right to free speech, winning himself the soubriquet of Philippe Égalité. On 30 June 1789, soldiers who days earlier had refused an order to shoot into a crowd of insurgents were freed from prison by the mob and led to the Palais-Royal, where they were protected and honoured as heroes.

In the days leading up to the revolution that July, the Palais-Royal cafés were fairly buzzing with sedition. Arthur Young, an Englishman visiting Paris at the time, described the scene:

> The coffee houses present yet more singular and astounding spectacles; they are not only crowded within, but other expectant crowds are at the doors and windows, listening to certain orators who from chairs or tables harangue each his little audience; the eagerness with which they are heard, and the thunder of applause they receive for every sentiment of violence against the government, cannot easily be imagined.

On Sunday, 12 July, the journalist Camille Desmoulins rushed out of the Café de Foy, leapt on to one of the pavement tables and began an impassioned speech. He'd been particularly incensed by the sudden dismissal the previous day of the finance minister, Jacques Necker, a popular reformer who was against despotism and believed in a constitutional monarchy. Now Desmoulins exhorted the crowd surging around him to take up arms. With a pistol in one hand and sword in the other, he shouted that the time to fight had come. In this first overt act of the French Revolution, he marched a thousand or so of his followers away to scour the city for arms.

Camille Desmoulins rousing the revolutionaries at the Café de Foy in Paris on 12 July 1789.

Two days later, the mob broke into the Hôtel des Invalides, where they seized the cannons and muskets stored in the cellars. From there they went on to storm the Bastille, the fortress prison and armoury, which stood as a symbol of the monarchy's dictatorial rule, and captured its store of gunpowder and ammunition.

And that's how Bastille Day, on 14 July, was born.

Lafayette, hero a decade earlier of the American Revolution, helped launch the French Revolution too and served in its National Assembly. On behalf of the people of France, he sent the key to the Bastille to George Washington, then serving as America's first president. It is still on display at Washington's Mount Vernon home.

The Procope continued to play an active role during the years of the revolution (in this period it was known as the Café Zoppi). It was where the Phrygian cap, that soft, red conical cap with the top bent forwards – the revolution's emblem of

Maximilien Robespierre.

Georges Danton.

liberty – was first worn. And the café was a gathering place for the Cordeliers Club, named after a Paris district closely associated with radicalism, whose full name was the Society of the Friends of the Rights of Man and of the Citizen. Desmoulins and Danton were leading lights of this political grouping, which campaigned for direct democracy and voting rights for all men. It was at the Procope that the order was given, on 10 August 1792, to attack the Tuileries Palace, the king's residence. The bloody insurrection, planned and executed with strong involvement from the Cordeliers, was the turning point of the revolution. It effectively abolished the monarchy and propelled France towards republicanism, with the establishment of the National Convention, the legislative body overseeing this mammoth change.

As time went on the Cordeliers tried to rein in the abuses of power by Robespierre and his ill-named Committee of Public Safety, whose tumbrils carried a never-ending stream of 'enemies of the revolution' to the guillotine. They called for an end to the Terror.

Camille Desmoulins.

As we know, bloody revolutions ultimately devour their own. Accused of conspiring to overthrow the National Convention, the Cordeliers Club was crushed, and in April 1794, Desmoulins and Danton were led to the guillotine. Three months later, Robespierre's head rolled too. The three revolutionaries lived only a scant year or so after the royal pair, Louis and Marie Antoinette. All five died in their thirties: short lives containing a surfeit of drama.

Novel events

The Procope entered a calmer period in the nineteenth century. By mid-century, there were at least 4,000 cafés in Paris, but due to its illustrious past, the Procope retained a certain cachet. It was the refuge of choice for some of France's most celebrated writers – George Sand, Victor Hugo, Alfred de Musset and occasionally, Honoré de Balzac (if Voltaire drank forty cups of coffee a day, Balzac was said to consume up to fifty, asserting that coffee was 'a great power' in his life).

In the 1860s, the café once again had a burst of political significance when it became the meeting place for a debating society called the Conférence Molé. Its purpose was to hold debates about legislation, administration, the economy and general politics, in order to train future politicians. The society also provided a means for young political hopefuls to rub shoulders with established political figures.

This is the period of the Second French Empire, the eighteen-year regime of Napoleon Bonaparte's nephew, Napoleon III, from 1852 to 1870, between the country's Second and Third Republic. (French history gets a bit convoluted around this time.) The society, moderately conservative and critical of the Second Empire's authoritarian regime, was nonetheless one of the few public places where a degree of free discussion was allowed. One of many French orators to learn the art of public speaking from the Conférence Molé meetings at the Procope was Léon Gambetta, the popular republican politician who proclaimed the Third Republic in 1870 and was prominent in its early government.

Towards the end of his life in the late nineteenth century the poet Paul Verlaine, Left Bank bohemian and leader of the *fin-de-siècle* Symbolist and Decadent artistic movements, made the Café Procope his haunt. Both the public and his peers admired his work, but he'd had some very shaky times. He abandoned his wife and son in favour of a tempestuous homosexual relationship with fellow poet Arthur Rimbaud (during which he fired shots at his lover in a drunken rage and was duly imprisoned).

Afterwards he spent some years in England, where he taught drawing and languages. Another love affair, with a French pupil, ended tragically with the young Frenchman's death from typhus. Eventually, Verlaine returned to Paris and descended into alcoholism, drug addiction and poverty. He lived in slums and spent his days drinking in cafés, but mostly in the Procope, where he sometimes liked to place himself at the hallowed marble table used by Voltaire during the previous century. There is a sad photograph of him sitting alone, leaning back against a banquette, a glass of red wine before him. His eyes are half closed and he hasn't bothered to take off his hat.

In 1895, Verlaine was elected *Prince des Poètes* – Prince of Poets – by the French literary world. But he paid a heavy price for his dissolute lifestyle and early the following year, at the age of 51, he died of pulmonary congestion. His funeral was attended by 5,000 mourners.

The American writer W.C. Morrow, in his book *Bohemian Paris of Today*, published in 1900, described the Procope at the close of the nineteenth century:

> Thc dim illumination is in perfect keeping with the other appointments of the place, which are dark, sombre and funereal. The woodwork, the chairs and the tables are deeply stained by time, the contrasting white marble tops of the tables suggesting gravestones; and with all these go the deeply discoloured walls.

Paul Verlaine at the Café Procope.

Napoleon's hat, left as security at the Café Procope.

Small wonder then, that in the early twentieth century the Procope slid downhill, becoming a modest restaurant frequented not by celebrities but by students and office workers. It was converted back into a café in the 1920s, when for a while it was known as Au Grand Soleil. But at some point, the owner, recognising the promotional value of its long and rich history, renamed it the Café Procope.

In 1989, it was lavishly refurbished in an eighteenth-century style, with crystal chandeliers and gilt-framed paintings of famous past patrons decorating the rich red walls. Much more extensive than in the old days, it has two plush storeys with numerous rooms for eating and drinking and reminders everywhere of its priceless historical associations. There are busts of Voltaire and Benjamin Franklin, commemorative plaques and quotes recalling the Enlightenment and heroes of the revolution, as well as display cabinets with historical documents. A reproduction of the 1789 Declaration of the Rights of Man and of the Citizen document hangs on a wall.

And in a hallway upstairs is Voltaire's marble-topped, slightly chipped writing desk, reputedly a gift from his close friend, Fredrick the Great of Prussia.

Also upstairs is a glass case containing Napoleon Bonaparte's bicorne hat. Legend has it that as a young, newly trained artillery officer during the revolution he would visit the Procope in search of a commission, though he was generally distracted into playing chess, a common pastime then in Parisian cafés. But he had perhaps already developed a penchant for coffee, which would stand him in good stead later as he set about conquering the world. 'Strong coffee, and plenty, awakens me,' he once remarked. 'It gives me a warmth, an unusual force, a pain that is not without pleasure. I would rather suffer than be senseless.'

On one occasion at the Procope, he was unable to pay for his food and drink and was forced to leave his hat as security. But how odd that he never returned at some point to collect it. Perhaps he decamped in a hurry to do battle. No one could have suspected at the time that the cash-strapped young army officer would end the French Revolution in 1799 by staging a coup d'état and appointing himself First Consul, let alone go on to crown himself Emperor – *Emperor!* – five years later.

The street on which Francesco Procopio opened his café nearly three and a half centuries ago is today called Rue de l'Ancienne Comédie, in memory of its former neighbour, the Comédie-Française. Whilst the theatre company moved to other premises a very long time ago, how gratifying it is that the Procope has stayed put. It may be more of a high-class restaurant now than a simple café, but alongside the fancy contemporary items on the menu are a few 'historic recipes'. For example, one can sit down and order *tête de veau en cocotte comme en 1686* (calf's head casserole, 1686 style) and feel *transporté* to the seventeenth century. Those who prefer the eighteenth century can choose from the 'Philosophers' Menu', or opt for the 'Revolutionaries beef fillet'.

Chapter Five

CAFFÈ FLORIAN, VENICE

It's no coincidence that the most famous medieval merchant-cum-explorer was the Venetian Marco Polo – for centuries during the Middle Ages the Republic of Venice was the most powerful and wealthiest mercantile centre in the world. It is even perceived as the birthplace of modern capitalism, the first hub of international finance. The sovereign maritime state dubbed La Serenissima (the Most Serene) lasted for 1,100 years from AD 697, and its success was due to its advantageous location on the Adriatic Sea, allowing its merchants to be the conduit between the Levant and the Middle East and destinations throughout Europe. Venice was the key port of entry for naval trade with the Arabs and the Turks for imports from the flourishing markets of Constantinople and Alexandria. And it was the end point of the fabled 5,000-mile Silk Road trade route from China.

We've already seen how coffee first reached Europe from the Ottoman Empire in the sixteenth century via the port of Venice. It arrived along with an array of luxury goods from the East – silk, glass, carpets, perfumes, jewellery, wines, caviar, marzipan, rock crystal … slaves too, of course, many of whom became gondoliers along the Venetian canals and lagoons. For a long time Venice had a monopoly in the lucrative salt market throughout the Italian peninsula, as well as monopolising the trade in spices from India. Shrewd and highly competitive, the republic's wealthy merchant class were the masters of Venice.

La Serenissima also had overseas and maritime possessions to safeguard its naval trade routes – the so-called *Domini da Mar* (Domains of the Sea) – including, at various times, parts of present-day Montenegro, Slovenia, Croatia, Albania, Greece and Cyprus. The entire republic was ruled by the Doge, or chief magistrate, elected by the members of the Great Council of Venice. This was a quasi-parliament, with membership restricted only to the patrician families included in the *Libro d'Oro* (*The Golden Book*), a directory of the Venetian nobles.

However, the opening of new trade routes via the Atlantic Ocean to the Americas and East Indies heralded Venice's decline as a maritime powerhouse. As trade shifted to the Atlantic, it became more and more difficult for Venice to establish trade monopolies and its international status waned. Gradually it lost its colonies, trading outposts and control of commercial activities in the Adriatic.

Evening carousing at Venice's Caffè Florian in the eighteenth century, painting by Alessandro Milesi.

After a series of wars between Venice and the Ottomans, the final war, from 1714 to 1718, ended disastrously for Venice with the loss of its most prized colony, Crete. But the treaty arranged with the intervention of the British and Dutch governments ushered in an era of peace for the Republic of Venice, which retained its continental Italian domain north of the Po Valley, extending almost to Milan. And its principal marketplace, the Rialto in the heart of Venice, continued to function as a financial and commercial centre, and focal point for the still influential merchant class.

In the eighteenth century, Venice entered a new phase in its history – the *Pax Venetiae*. Its maritime glories had faded along with its ageing palazzos, but it had transformed itself into a city state dedicated to the arts and culture, to sybaritic pleasures and public amusements, a scandalously lively social scene, theatricality, carnivals and masked balls – flamboyance. Café life was integral to it all and no café played a greater part than the Caffè Florian, which opened its doors beneath the arches of the Procuratie Nuove in the magnificent Piazza San Marco in 1720, at the dawn of this Venetian age of hedonism and sensuality. Its founder was Floriano Francesconi, who boldly named his café Venezia Trionfante (Venice Triumphant). But perhaps because that sounded rather pretentious, everyone soon named it after him. Caffè Florian started out as two plainly furnished rooms – a far cry from the extensive and lavish establishment of today (the result of, firstly, a mid-nineteenth-century revamp, and a further refurbishment in the late twentieth century).

From the beginning, the café was a great success, due in large part to the character of Floriano himself; he was a well-liked proprietor and endlessly obliging towards his patrons. He was also a mine of social information regarding the denizens of Venice – in effect, a human 'city directory' – and the trusted acquaintance of hundreds. Inhabitants travelling away from Venice left their itineraries with him, and those arriving from elsewhere asked him for news about the Venetians they wished to see. The British bibliographer William Carew Hazlitt said of Floriano in his 1905 book, *The Venetian Republic*: 'He long concentrated in himself a knowledge more varied and multifarious than that possessed by any individual before or since.'

Playwright of the people

Artists and writers, philosophers and poets, aristocrats and adventurers frequented the Caffè Florian; it became the favoured watering hole of the Venetian elite and in due course doubled in size. One famous regular was the playwright and librettist Carlo Goldoni. He'd been educated as a lawyer and held lucrative legal positions but in the 1730s, still a young man, he changed his career and devoted himself to writing plays and managing theatres. After a failed early attempt at a tragic play, he discovered that his true talent lay in comedy. But he was eager to break away from the conventional comic form in Italy at the time, the *commedia dell'arte*, part-improvised works featuring stock characters – Harlequin, Pantalone, Pulcinella et al. – wearing their customary masks and costumes. What he had in mind were works that held up a mirror to contemporary society, reflecting with candour and wit the lives of the people around him and their values, foibles, discords and manners. He made rich use of the Venetian vernacular, a regional language distinct from the standardised Tuscan Italian, which came from Florence. This innovative approach kick-started a revolution in Italian theatre.

As an enthusiast of coffee and cafés, it's not surprising that Goldoni drew inspiration from them. His play *La Bottega del Caffè* (*The Coffee House*), first

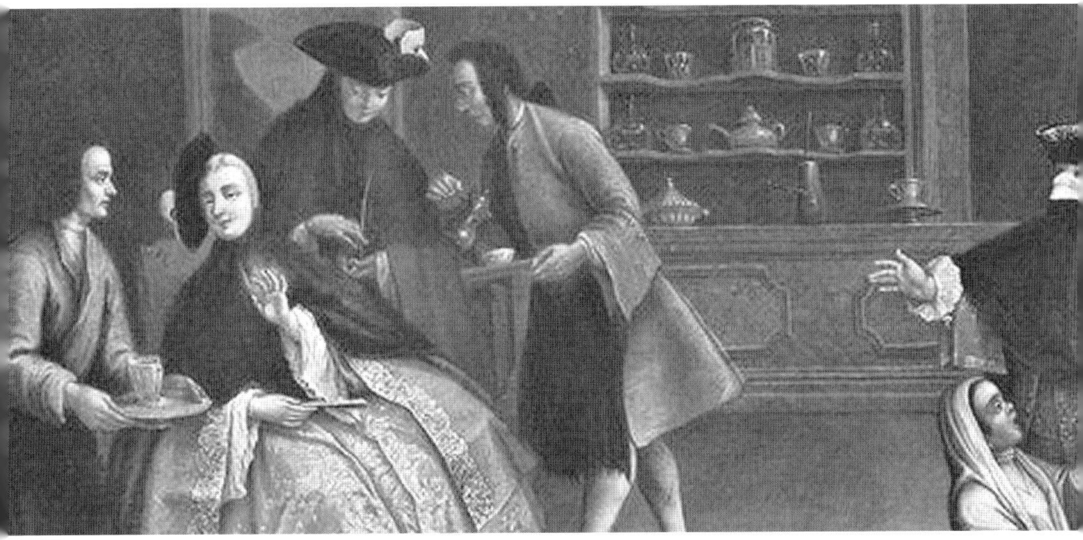

An illustration for Carlo Goldoni's play, *The Coffee House*.

performed in 1750, was a naturalistic comedy of bourgeois Venice, set in and around a Venetian coffee house clearly modelled on Florian's. It's a microcosm where different characters interact, including a gambler, a dancer, a cloth merchant, a waiter, a disgraceful Neapolitan nobleman, and of course Ridolfo, the coffee shop owner, 'a man of great kindness' no doubt based on Floriano Francesconi. They get involved in each other's affairs, creating conflicts aplenty, but Ridolfo smooths them all out in the end.

In his verse play *La Sposa Persiana* (*The Persian Wife*) Goldoni illustrates the art of coffee making in the eighteenth century. The female character of Curcuma, custodian of a harem, explains to her charges:

> Here is the coffee, ladies, coffee native of Arabia,
> and carried by the caravans into Isfahan.
> The coffee of Arabia is certainly always the best.
> While putting forth its leaves on one side,
> upon the other the flowers appear.
> Born of a rich soil, it wishes shade, or but little sun.
> Planted every three years is this little tree in the surface of the soil.
> The fruit, though truly very small,
> should yet grow large enough to become somewhat green.
> Later, when used, it should be freshly ground.
> Kept in a warm and dry place and jealously guarded.
> But a small quantity is needed to prepare it.

Put in the desired quantity and do not spill it over the fire.
Heat it till the foam rises, then let it subside again away from the fire.
Do this seven times at least, and coffee is made in a moment.

Goldoni was a humanist whose plays promoted moral and civic values, honour and integrity, and abjured arrogance, intolerance and the abuse of power. He believed in the importance of the emerging middle class as a corrective to both high-born privilege and low-born deprivation. Today, he's best known for his classic, *Il Servitore di Due Padroni* (*The Servant of Two Masters*), translated and adapted many times. The English playwright Richard Bean's adaptation, *One Man, Two Guvnors*, was a hit at London's National Theatre in 2011, later transferring to Broadway.

Changing fortunes for the Gozzi brothers

Cafés became the centre of social, commercial and intellectual life in Italian cities in the eighteenth century, and quickly multiplied. They were where people went to discuss politics and do business. Tellingly, the name given to the foremost intellectual journal published in Italian during this period was *Il Caffè*. It was founded in Milan by the aristocratic brothers Counts Pietro and Alessandro Verri, who modelled it on Joseph Addison and Richard Steele's *Spectator*. Although short-lived (from 1764 to 1766), it was instrumental in spreading the ideals of the Enlightenment throughout the Italian peninsula.

But Venice also had its erudite periodicals and two of them were produced in the early 1760s by the writer Count Gasparo Gozzi: *La Gazzetta Veneta*, a chronicle of Venetian life full of lively stories and skits, and *L'Osservatore*, a more serious literary journal. Gozzi too was influenced by the English journalistic style of *The Spectator*, and his prolific output encompassed prose and poetry, book and theatre reviews, philosophical essays, satires and character sketches. He soon earned a reputation as a gifted critic and elegant literary stylist. Not only were the many hours Gozzi spent at the Caffè Florian a rich source of material and inspiration for his writing, the café was also one of the few places where members of the public could buy *La Gazzetta Veneta* and *L'Osservatore*, thanks to benevolent owner Floriano's offer to help promote his ventures.

The eighteenth-century Venetian writer Gasparo Gozzi.

Gasparo Gozzi was the eldest of eleven children from a once-wealthy noble family that had fallen on hard times. The Swiss writer Philippe

Monnier describes Gasparo and his huge, insolvent family most entertainingly in his book *Venice in the Eighteenth Century*. As their creditors clamour to be paid, it seems the Gozzis all aspire to make money from writing, as they bustle about:

> in their dilapidated old palazzo rising out of the unclean water, with its doors hanging by their hinges, its floor falling in, and the cobwebs trailing from the rafters ... And everywhere ink stains! Always some scheme for an article, a play or a novel to be drafted, or for some prospective lawsuit. The tables are covered with a mixture of summonses and sonnets, both alike nibbled by the mice ... A strange crowd coming and going on the stairs, where bailiffs, money-lenders, lawyers, broken-down playwrights, old ladies with baskets, persons with ideas and starveling wits, shoulder each other. Everybody is looking for a rhyme.

Whilst Gasparo achieved fame with his journalism, later published in book form, and became a respected government official dealing with cultural policy and supervising printed works, his brother Carlo became a celebrated dramatist. He authored many plays and theatrical works known as *fiabe teatrali* – fantasies based on fairy tales and fables – and was a champion of traditional *commedia dell'arte*. His bitter falling out with the realist Carlo Goldoni over their conflicting theatrical preferences led to the latter's abandonment of Venice. In 1761, Goldoni moved to Paris, where he was put in charge of the Théâtre-Italien. He spent the rest of his life in France, writing mostly in French.

Hijinks and low points for Casanova

Fascinatingly, the streets of Venice were themselves a kind of theatre, where all manner of intrigues were played out. As Philippe Monnier writes:

> There are all sorts of nooks and corners and hiding places; the city is full of staircases, secret doors and clandestine abodes ... In this maze of canals, this labyrinth of lanes, you might play a splendid game of hide-and-seek. Venice is the ideal city for adventures, a home for the adventurer.

And there was no greater adventurer than the arch libertine Giacomo Casanova – high-stakes gambler, occultist, violinist, Freemason, traveller, debtor, duellist, spy, periodic lawyer, soldier and clergyman, escaped convict, and arguably the most inexhaustible lover of women the world has ever seen. For Casanova, whose sole concern was to satisfy his desires at all costs, Venice seemed perfect.

Venetians were renowned for their love of beautiful women and the city abounded with them. Some were courtesans, some belonged to the patrician families of *The Golden Book*, and others were nuns or peasant girls or workmen's daughters. There was a lot of illicit sex going on, filling the state orphanages with the resultant offspring. But even in this highly charged sexual environment, Casanova's legendary carnal exploits were in a class of their own. His liaisons frequently had their beginnings in the cafés of the Piazza San Marco, with the Caffè Florian chief among them – a useful hunting ground, as for a time it was the only café to admit women. (In 1767, the Venetian government banned women from cafés over concerns about immorality and public decency, but courtesans and noblewomen alike rejected the attempt to limit their freedom and ignored the ban. Nevertheless, the state kept a watchful eye on cafés, which they regarded as 'social cankers', by posting spies in them.)

Casanova was born in 1725, the eldest of six children of an itinerant actress and an actor. His father died when he was 8 and he was brought up by his grandmother and a guardian. Intelligent and inquisitive, he was interested in studying medicine. But on his guardian's advice, when he entered the University of Padua at the age of 12 it was to study law – for which he later claimed to have 'an unconquerable aversion'. Back in Venice, he managed through his charm and wit to ingratiate himself with Alvise Malipiero, a wealthy 76-year-old senator and owner of the imposing Palazzo Malipiero, near Casanova's own home in Venice. Malipiero became his patron, introducing him to the top people and teaching him about fine food and wines and the correct way to behave in high society. The ageing connoisseur and the eager-to-learn teenager enjoyed each other's company so much that Casanova became a daily visitor to the palazzo and attended his patron's elegant soirées and garden parties. However, it all came to a sticky end when Malipiero caught him flirting with the young actress whom he himself hoped to seduce. Both were unceremoniously booted out.

Not long afterwards, aged 17, Casanova lost his virginity to two high-born sisters, Nanetta and Marta Savorgnan, then 14 and 16. He found himself alone one evening with the agreeable pair, and after sharing two bottles of wine and a dinner of smoked meats, bread and cheese, they enjoyed a long night of 'ever varied skirmishes'. And so his career as the great seducer took off. By now, the tall and striking teenager was quite the dandy, with his long hair powdered, scented and elaborately curled. He had grudgingly begun a legal career, as well as taking holy orders as a minor clergyman (to please his guardian), but much of his time was spent gambling, chasing women and enjoying a dynamic social life at fashionable haunts such as the Florian.

When this dissolute lifestyle brought sufficient opprobrium to curtail his pet pastimes, he decided to enlist as an officer in the Venetian army. He acquired a snazzy white uniform decorated with silver and gold, a hat with a black cockade, a long sword and 'handsome cane', and joined a regiment at Corfu. But he found his advancement too slow and his duties boring, and he lost his army pay in a card game. He thus abandoned his military career, returned to Venice and began yet another profession, as violinist in a theatre orchestra. Realising he didn't excel at the instrument and therefore took no pride in his playing, he threw himself into endless hijinks with his 'degraded fellow musicians'. With little sign of contrition, he later recalled:

> We often spent our nights roaming through different quarters of the city, thinking up the most scandalous practical jokes and putting them into execution … we amused ourselves by untying the gondolas moored before private homes, which then drifted with the current.

Like naughty schoolboys, they also sent midwives and physicians on false alarms.

Then, out of the blue, at the age of 21 he had a stroke of good luck (not unusual for him). He had been playing the violin at a wedding party and was leaving his orchestra to return home, when he paused to pick up a letter unknowingly dropped by one of the guests, Senator Matteo Bragadin. After Casanova returned the letter to him, a grateful Bragadin offered him a ride home in the gondola he had just boarded. Three minutes later, as the two men sat side by side in the gondola, the senator suffered a stroke. Casanova acted quickly, halting the boat and hurrying to fetch a doctor, who immediately bled the afflicted man. Once the trio arrived at the senator's home, Palazzo Bragadin di Santa Marina, his own physician was summoned. But there was a problem. The physician treated his patient by applying to his chest a mercury poultice, and the toxic concoction induced a dangerously high fever, which Casanova sensed might actually be killing him. What's more, Bragadin appeared to be choking on his own swollen windpipe. Dismissing the doctor's protests, Casanova ordered the removal of the poultice and the washing down of the senator's chest with cool water.

After a rest, Bragadin slowly began to recover and hailed his new young friend as a saviour, wise beyond his years and evidently a master in the 'cabalistic arts'. After this episode, he regularly consulted Casanova on all esoteric matters and invited him into his household, adopting him as his son. Casanova was provided with accommodation, food, his own servant and gondola, and a monthly stipend. Thus, at a single stroke (pardon the pun), Casanova's status was changed from that of impecunious mischief-making violinist to palazzo-residing gentleman, dressed in the finest attire, free to gamble and pursue his amorous escapades.

As Casanova later noted: 'I should have been allowed to do as I wished and become a physician, in which profession quackery is even more effective than it is in legal practice.'

Bragadin became his devoted long-term patron, bound to him by affection and gratitude, though at times this devotion was sorely tested. In the following years Casanova's outrageous antics (his practical jokes included digging up a newly buried corpse) and sexual improprieties kept getting him into trouble with the authorities and forcing him temporarily to flee Venice. He took off and spent time in Paris, Dresden, Prague and Vienna, seducing the ladies wherever he went.

When Casanova finally returned to Venice in 1753 he resumed his old ways, but the Venetian Inquisitors, responsible for stamping out public debauchery, now employed a spy to report on him. He had a lengthening police record of reported blasphemies, seductions, fights and other controversies, and an anxious Bragadin warned him to leave the city once more, before the net closed in. He ignored the warning.

Midnight flight

Casanova's luck ran out one night in 1755, shortly after his thirtieth birthday, when the police burst into his bedroom. Prosecuted for being a cardsharp, con man, Freemason, cabbalist and blasphemer – in short, an affront to the Catholic religion and common decency – he was sentenced to five years' imprisonment in the attic cells known as the Leads, beneath the lead roof of the Doge's Palace.

There he languished for fifteen months, until making a daring escape with a fellow prisoner, a disgraced monk. Using a sharpened metal bar they made holes in the ceiling and climbed on to the roof. With the help of a rope made from their bedding and the lucky discovery of a workman's ladder, they lowered themselves down the sloping lead plates and reached the parapet. Casanova prised open a dormer window and they entered a room where they waited until early morning. Then they changed into some smarter clothes they'd taken along, broke a lock on an exit door and entered a palace corridor. Walking through various rooms and galleries, and down the grand staircase, they headed to the main entrance, where they convinced the guards they'd been accidentally locked in after an official function the night before, and stepped out to freedom – the only prisoners ever to escape the Leads. They departed the city by gondola, and Casanova headed to Paris.

In France he made friends in high places (with Madame de Pompadour, no less, and Rousseau), found work as a spy and bounced around Europe on various missions. He got involved in dodgy business ventures, gambled away his money and was chased for his debts, spent more time in prison, and enjoyed countless liaisons with *les femmes*. In 1763, he washed up in England, hoping to sell his idea of a state lottery to English officials. Though his connections secured him an audience with King George III, it led nowhere. Meanwhile, his usual bedroom shenanigans landed him with venereal disease. He left England penniless and ill.

Dunkirk, Cologne, Stuttgart, Marseilles, Moscow, St Petersburg, Warsaw, Dresden, Barcelona … the nomadic seducer spent time in them all, for one reason or another. At last, after eighteen years of exile, the Venetian Inquisitors permitted him to return home. But things were not the same. Now middle-aged and looking fairly ragged, he'd lost his easy-going, debonair manner, and willing females were thin on the ground. His indulgent patron, Bragadin, had died. Casanova did some spying work for the Inquisitors, and endeavoured to make his mark as a writer. However, when he penned a malicious satire on the Venetian nobility, he was once again expelled from Venice and forced to resume his wanderings.

Painting of Giacomo Casanova, by Francesco Narici, 1760.

His final years were spent in Bohemia (now the Czech Republic), residing at Dux Castle, where he was employed as librarian to Count Joseph Karl von Waldstein. The job was well paid but dull, and as a consummate man-about-town, he wasn't thrilled to be based in such a backwater. So he busied himself by writing his memoirs, in French. It's not surprising that, having packed so much extraordinary living into his life, he produced one of the longest autobiographies ever written. *Histoire de Ma Vie* (*The History of My Life*) comprises twelve volumes – some 3,500 pages, or 1.2 million words.

Casanova died in 1798 at the age of 73. He was the ultimate creation of eighteenth-century Venice – its clandestine abodes, secret doors and staircases, its maze of canals and labyrinth of lanes, its flamboyance, its love of masks and carnivals, its sexiness and its pulsating café life.

Canova carves a foot, Goethe collects seashells

Much-loved proprietor Floriano Francesconi ran his establishment in St Mark's Square with great success for decades; it was a beacon to the great minds and talents of Venice and beyond. Amongst other notables, it was frequented by Jean-Jacques Rousseau in 1743–4, when the philosopher worked as secretary to the French ambassador to Venice, Comte de Montaigu. The Florian no doubt offered a comforting bolthole from his job, as it was an unhappy assignment. His miserly aristocratic boss never paid him on time, and when Rousseau quit after eleven months the experience left him with a distaste for government bureaucracy.

Later on, the now elderly Floriano was friend and benefactor to Antonio Canova, an up-and-coming young sculptor. The son of a stonemason, Canova had learnt how to carve marble by the age of 9 and won numerous prizes as a teenage student at the Accademia di Belle Arti di Venezia. Floriano was suffering from gout, and in return for the café owner's kindness towards him, Canova came to his aid when he needed to buy new shoes. He carved a model of Floriano's foot so that the shoemaker could take his measurements without inflicting any pain on the elderly gent. Canova went on to achieve international fame as a great Neoclassical sculptor of marble statues, perhaps most notably his masterpiece, *The Three Graces*.

Floriano finally retired in 1773 and his grandson, Valentino Francesconi, took over the business. In the following decade, the café was visited by another of the era's luminaries, German polymath and author of the classic play *Faust*, Johann Wolfgang von Goethe. Granted a paid leave of absence from his duties as Privy Councillor in the Duchy of Weimar, in 1786–8 he made an extended tour of the Italian peninsula and Sicily, a long-held ambition. It proved to be of great significance in his artistic development.

During his fortnight in Venice, Goethe admired the Renaissance architecture of Palladio's church of Santa Maria della Carità, writing in his diary: 'I have never seen anything more sublime, more perfect, in my life.' And he went to see a Goldoni play, *Le Baruffe Chiozzotte* (*Brawling in Chioggia*), which he thoroughly enjoyed. The plot centres on two women who love the same man, giving rise to comic struggles and outrageous behaviour between two groups of fishermen in Chioggia, a village on an island at the entrance to the Venetian Lagoon. 'At last I have seen a real comedy!' declared Goethe, who considered Goldoni a genius of the theatre.

Before leaving Venice, Goethe took a solitary walk along the Lido, the long barrier island in the Lagoon. Listening to the splashing waves, picking up seashells to take home to his children in Weimar, he absorbed the unique atmosphere of La Serenissima. His diary entry for the day concluded: 'Venice can only be compared to itself.' The diary was published many years later as *Italian Journey*.

One year after Goethe's return from Venice, the French Revolution broke out and the Venetian government feared that its radical ideas might spread to its own territory. The Florian, with customers from all over Europe, became a meeting point for many French revolutionaries, so the State Inquisitors forced Valentino Francesconi to shut it down for a while.

The café hospital

It was all change in 1797, when the French armies entered Venice led by Napoleon Bonaparte. The decade-long wars between the monarchic powers of Europe – a consequence of the French Revolution – brought about the dissolution and dismemberment of the Republic of Venice. On 12 May, Ludovico Manin, the last Doge of Venice, formally abolished the republic after 1,100 years of existence. The French proceeded to loot Venice and either requisition or sink all the ships of the Venetian navy, a final humiliation for what had been one of the world's foremost maritime empires. In a secret treaty with the Austrians, Napoleon gave them Venice, and it was duly incorporated into the Austrian Habsburg Empire.

The Caffè Florian continued to thrive. In 1814, Valentino passed the business on to his son, Antonio. The next major episode in which the café played a role was in 1848–9, when Europe was convulsed by anti-Habsburg revolutions (more about this in a later chapter), and Venice too tried to free itself from Austrian domination. The 'Senate Room' of the Florian was the gathering place for a party of patriotic Venetians who helped bring about the self-declared Republic of San Marco, based in Venice and its surrounding region of Venetia. During the fighting against Austrian forces the Florian took in wounded Venetian insurgents, becoming a temporary hospital. Alas, the Italian revolutionary state of San Marco existed for only seventeen months until, following a long siege, it was reconquered by the Austrian army.

Famous names in the guestbook

In 1858, the venerable Caffè Florian at last left family hands. Antonio Francesconi sold it to a group of businessmen, and the new owners carried out restoration work and extensive interior redecoration, creating an opulent mélange of gilding and mirrors, frescos and elaborate stuccowork. Nevertheless, the venue retained its appeal to artists and writers. Henry James enthused about Venice in the later decades of the nineteenth century in his travel book, *Italian Hours*:

> There is no simpler pleasure than looking at a fine Titian … or than floating in a gondola or than hanging over a balcony or than taking one's coffee at Florian's. It is of such superficial pastimes that a Venetian day is composed, and the pleasure of the matter is in the emotions to which they minister.

Early in the next century, Thomas Mann's summer holiday at the Grand Hôtel des Bain on the Venice Lido gave rise to his famous novella, *Death in Venice*. It was adapted into Luchino Visconti's 1971 film of the same name, starring Dirk Bogarde. The story concerned an ageing writer's fixation with a beautiful 14-year-old Polish boy on holiday with his family at the very same Grand Hôtel des Bain. Mann himself had been enthralled by an angelic-looking Polish youngster there, and the melancholy tale was a reflection of his inner struggles with homosexuality.

Both Thomas Mann and Gustav von Aschenbach, the writer in the story, patronised the Florian: 'In mid-afternoon [Aschenbach] took the vaporetto across the stale-smelling lagoon to Venice. He got out at San Marco, took tea on the Piazza and then … set off on a walk through the streets.' We can be fairly certain Mann is referring to the Florian, where tea is taken on the Piazza, as the writer was a

Caffè Florian in the nineteenth century, painting by Italico Brass.

familiar figure there during his stay in 1911, and his signature appears in one of the café's guestbooks.

In our own time, we almost lost this irreplaceable historic treasure. In November 2019, following heavy rain and high tides, Venice suffered its worst flooding for fifty years and the Piazza San Marco became a lake 3 feet deep. The Florian was badly damaged and was just getting back on its feet when the Covid pandemic struck – and most inopportunely, in the year of the café's 300th anniversary, 2020. Lockdowns turned the normally tourist-filled city into a ghost town and over the next two years, the Florian lost so much income it was on the brink of bankruptcy. Thankfully, the oldest café in Italy was saved from closure with a little help from the Italian government, and the determination of the Venetian company that owns it to keep it going.

There aren't many cities that you can say have hardly changed since the eighteenth century, but if the statement applies anywhere, it's Venice. La Serenissima has made few concessions to our modern epoch – no cars, no traffic jams, just gondolas floating silently on the canals. If Casanova were to make a comeback today, he would have no problem negotiating his way around his hometown … as long as he doesn't come when a gargantuan cruise ship has just disgorged thousands of day-trippers.

Chapter Six

CAFFÈ ANTICO GRECO, ROME

Italy's second oldest café after the Florian is the Caffè Antico Greco, in the Eternal City, Rome. It was founded in 1760 by Nicola della Maddalena, a Greek from the Levantine, hence the café's name. From the beginning, it was a gathering place for intellectuals of all kinds, especially artists, poets and writers. It is very well located, on the Via dei Condotti, which leads out from the Piazza di Spagna, at the bottom of the Spanish Steps. From the nineteenth century on, this piazza would be a hub for English and American ex-pats and even acquire the epithet of the 'English ghetto'.

Today, the Caffè Antico Greco's series of intimate, interconnecting rooms contains a treasure trove of gilt-framed paintings, drawings, photographs, letters

An eighteenth-century etching of the Piazza di Spagna, by Giovanni Battista Piranesi, showing Keats's apartment at far right.

and other relics linked to the illustrious regulars who in bygone centuries took refreshment there with their friends and associates.

The place has always had a clear direction of its own. In 1806, Napoleon imposed the continental blockade, preventing all ships from Britain or her colonies entering any port under French control. The policy, as intended, severely damaged Britain's economy, but ultimately backfired. France's revenue from customs fell and the European nations were starved of British colonial goods: sugar, tobacco, cocoa, cotton textiles … and coffee. Prices shot up. With the sharp rise in the cost of coffee, the café owners of Rome tried to keep the price of a cup of coffee constant by mixing chickpea, soya, chestnut or chicory flour in with the expensive coffee powder. Caffè Greco, however, carried on using only the pure kind. They doubled the price of a cup, and the cup became smaller, but the inimitable aroma of the genuine article continued to pull in the customers. By then, the Italians had developed their renowned connoisseurship with regard to the brew.

The Romantics

Italy has always exerted an irresistible attraction for our Romantic poets, due perhaps to a combination of the enchantment of the ruins of Ancient Rome, the splendour of the art and architecture of the Renaissance, and the gloriously un-English weather. 'Italia! O Italia! thou who hast the fatal gift of beauty,' wrote Lord Byron in *Childe Harold's Pilgrimage*, describing Rome as the 'city of the soul'. Percy Bysshe Shelley called Italy 'a paradise of exiles'.

By a curious stroke of fate, all three great Romantic poets – Byron, Shelley and John Keats – were in Italy in the early 1820s. Byron spent the years 1816 to 1823 there before setting off to Greece to support the natives in their War of Independence against the Ottoman Turks, dying there in 1824. Shelley was in Italy from 1818, before drowning four years later in a boating accident in the bay of La Spezia. Meanwhile, the ailing Keats spent the last few months of his short life in Rome, lodging in an apartment at the foot of the Spanish Steps, where he died of tuberculosis in February 1821 (the apartment is now part of the Keats-Shelley House museum). One thing they all did, though not together, was stop in at the Caffè Greco.

When Byron left England he was fleeing a failed relationship, huge debts and scandalous love affairs (so far, so Casanova). He never went back, embarking instead on his own version of the Grand Tour – the lengthy and languid journey around the continent of Europe so beloved of British nobles and landed gentry in the eighteenth and early nineteenth centuries. He spent the summer of 1816 renting a villa at Lake Geneva with Shelley, his wife Mary and Mary's teenage stepsister, Claire Clairmont, with whom Byron had already had a dalliance leading to the birth early the following year of their daughter. It was during that excessively wet, stormy summer, when the visiting Brits were trapped indoors with so little to do, that Mary Shelley wrote her classic novel, *Frankenstein*.

Afterwards, Byron travelled on to Italy, and in the spring of 1817 spent three weeks in Rome. He lodged at Piazza di Spagna 66, on the opposite side of the square from the house at No. 26, to which Keats would later move. As Byron's lodgings were even closer to the Caffè Greco, it's no wonder he went there. As well as Genoa, Pisa and later Ravenna, Byron spent three years in Venice (where it was the Caffè Florian that caught his fancy).

The trio of the Shelleys and Claire Clairmont – at times a tempestuous *ménage à trois* – also lived in various Italian cities before setting up home in Pisa, where Byron joined them in 1821. The two poets, by now firm friends, adored Italy's culture and literature (both became proficient in the Italian language), believing the country offered greater tolerance and freedom than England. Together with the critic and editor Leigh Hunt, who briefly joined them in Italy, they produced a short-lived, radical quarterly journal, *The Liberal*.

The intriguing thing about the friendship between Byron and Shelley was how utterly different the two poets were. Shelley was an idealist and optimist, whilst Byron's nature was darker, more fatalistic. Their daily habits were in stark contrast too – Byron was a night owl and Shelley an early riser, and tragically, whilst Byron loved swimming, Shelley couldn't swim …

Besides their literary bonds, their complex personal lives were intertwined. Claire had made the agonising decision that she couldn't raise her illegitimate daughter, who would be better off with the aristocratic Byron. So when the child was fifteen months old, Claire turned her over to him in Venice, explaining in a letter: 'I have sent you my child because I love her too well to keep her.' Byron changed their daughter's name from Alba to Allegra and placed her with foster families. Later, when he had left Venice and was living in Ravenna, he put her into a Catholic convent outside the city, where the little girl died at the age of 5, of either typhus or malaria. Claire never forgave him.

Shelley and his wife Mary knew only too well about the tragedy of losing a child, and likewise in Italy. Their toddler daughter Clara died of dysentery in Venice in 1818, and their son William was not much older when he died of malaria in Rome the following year. Only their second son, Percy Florence Shelley, was to live into adulthood.

The Shelleys, with Claire in tow, moved to Rome in March 1819. They rented lodgings on the fashionable Corso, near the Piazza Colonna. Though Shelley was an atheist, they attended services at St Peter's Basilica, home to Michelangelo's masterpiece, the *Pietà* sculpture. Shelley was captivated by the legends of Ancient Rome and the ruins around them. Again and again, he would visit the Forum and the Colosseum, though he was most enthralled by the Baths of Caracalla – they were then overgrown with foliage but bits of ancient mosaics could still be picked up from the dirt. Inspired by the surroundings, he sat there with notebook and pen, composing his verse play *Prometheus Unbound*. Published in 1820, his preface to the lyrical drama explained:

> This Poem was chiefly written upon the mountainous ruins of the Baths of Caracalla, among the flowery glades, and thickets of odiferous blossoming trees, which are extending in ever-winding labyrinths upon its immense platforms and dizzy arches suspended in the air. The bright blue sky of Rome, and the effect of the vigorous awakening of spring in that divinest climate, and the new life with which it drenches the spirits even to intoxication, were the inspiration of this drama.

In May, the Shelley party moved to lodgings in the Via Sestina, near the sixteenth-century Trinità dei Monti church at the top of the Spanish Steps. The following month tragedy struck with the death of their son William. He was buried in the Protestant Cemetery, just outside the old city walls, and only days later, the distraught Shelleys left Rome. The memory of it was too painful perhaps, for they never went back … not until Mary returned a few years on to inter her husband's ashes in their son's grave. To her shock, when the grave was opened the bones inside were those of an adult, not a small child, and no one could say where little William's remains were buried. It remains a mystery.

A posthumous life

Keats went to Italy in a last, desperate hope that the balmier climate would benefit his health and perhaps cure his consumption. He had wanted one of his good friends to accompany him on this sojourn but everyone he approached either couldn't or wouldn't agree to spending several months in Italy. In the end, his acquaintance, a good-natured young painter called Joseph Severn, agreed to be his companion. As an artist, Severn had longed to visit Italy, and he admired Keats, who at the age of 24 had already published three books of poetry (though they were derided by literary critics).

On 15 November 1820, they moved into the second-floor apartment at 26 Piazza di Spagna, where Severn proceeded to care for Keats with exemplary dedication. The poet became a patient of the Scottish physician James Clark, who had his well-established medical practice in the same piazza, at the heart of Rome's English-speaking community. Clark believed that Keats's ailments were caused by digestive problems, not tuberculosis, so instead of rest he prescribed exercise. Accordingly, in the early part of his stay, Keats spent time outdoors and was able to explore the surrounding area.

It would be hard to believe he didn't at some point take modest refreshment at the Caffè Greco, a stone's throw from his apartment, and he managed to climb the Spanish Steps to the Pincian Hill for gentle strolls through the landscaped park of the Villa Borghese. He even went horse riding on the hill with a young English army officer, Lieutenant Elton, who likewise suffered from tuberculosis. From the parapet before the Trinità dei Monti, he liked to savour the sweeping views of Rome at sunset – the glowing red Renaissance rooftops, the steeples, and in the distance the dome of St Peter's Basilica. He bought a few Italian books and studied the language.

Within a few weeks, however, his condition deteriorated so severely that all outdoor activities were impossible and he became a prisoner of the apartment. Tormented by thoughts of his unfulfilled life and impending death, he could no longer write poetry. He spent his final two months lying in his small bedroom overlooking the piazza and listening to its sounds – the trickling water in Bernini's Baroque-style fountain, the clopping of horses' hooves, the voices of fruit sellers and passers-by – as he coughed up blood from his shattered lungs.

Severn suspected that Clark's medical treatments were in fact hastening his friend's death. The doctor put him on a starvation diet to reduce the blood flow to his stomach, and, as was commonplace at the time, bled him – a combination that only weakened Keats the more. Daily he agonised, 'How long will this posthumous life of mine last?'

Severn nursed him devotedly, day and night, but on 23 February 1821, Keats died in his arms. His last words were: 'Severn, lift me up – I am dying – I shall die easy; don't be frightened – be firm, and thank God it has come.'

John Keats on his deathbed in Rome, drawn by his friend, Joseph Severn.

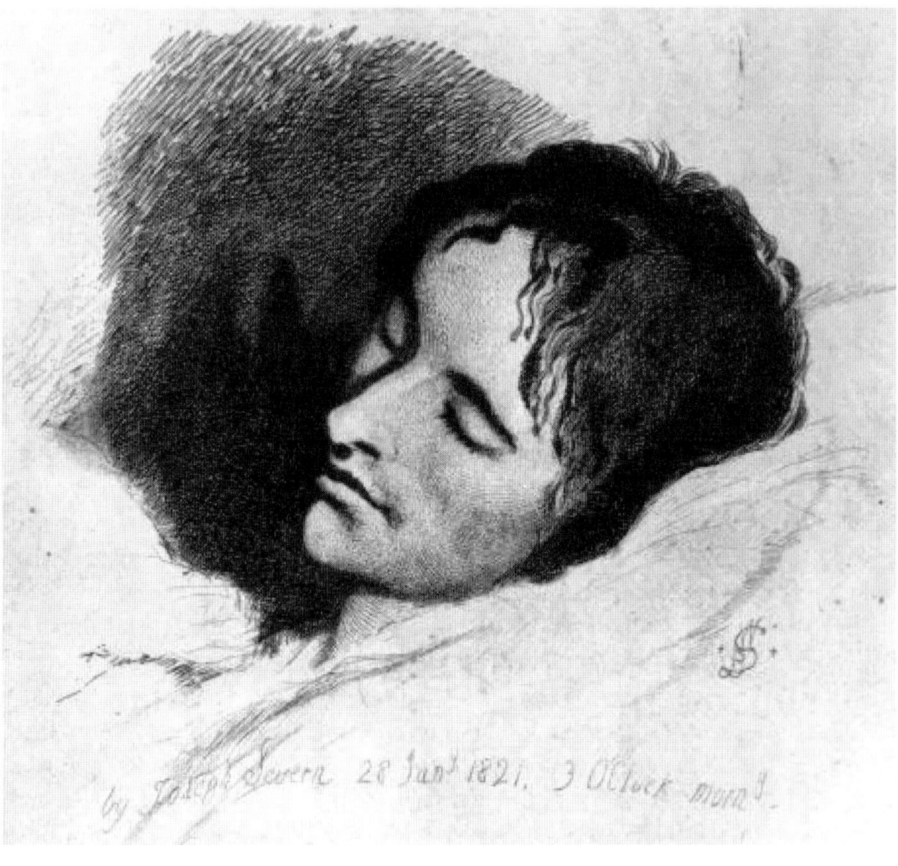

'He died so quiet, that I still thought he slept,' Severn wrote to a friend.

Convinced that nothing of his work would prove of lasting value, Keats had told Severn he wanted no name or date on his tombstone, only the words: 'Here lies one whose name was writ in water.'

After Keats's death Shelley wrote, by way of tribute, one of his finest poems, *Adonais; An Elegy on the Death of John Keats*. When in the summer of the following year Shelley's drowned body washed up on the Ligurian coast near Viareggio, it was in part identified by a book of Keats's poetry found in his jacket pocket. The graves of both poets lie in Rome's Protestant Cemetery. On his visit to Rome in 1877, Oscar Wilde prostrated himself on the grass before Keats's grave and called it the city's 'holiest place'. He later wrote a sonnet, 'The Grave of Keats', to commemorate the occasion. By then, far from being 'writ in water', the name Keats had begun to achieve the worldwide renown it carries today.

Side by side

Next to Keats lies the grave of his faithful friend, Joseph Severn, whose life in Rome by no means ended with the poet's death. He stayed on and launched a successful artistic career there, painting miniatures, landscapes and frescoes of historical and religious scenes. He also painted scenes of Italian peasant life, which proved popular with British visitors, bringing him many commissions, and he helped found the British Academy of the Fine Arts in Rome. However, on his return to England in 1841 he fell on hard times and was unable to earn sufficient money with his painting to support his growing family. In the end, like Byron and Casanova, he had to flee his creditors.

Luckily, a second career was waiting around the corner, for which he had his extensive Roman background to thank. In 1861, Severn was appointed British Consul in Rome, during the ferment over Italian unification – the *Risorgimento*. The revolutionary general Giuseppe Garibaldi had seized the Kingdom of Naples, and southern Italy and Sicily had been annexed to the new Kingdom of Italy. Most of the Italian peninsula's kingdoms, principalities and dukedoms had come together under the leadership of King Victor Emmanuel II, the first leader of an independent, united Italy since the days of the Roman Empire. Rome itself, however, was an outlier, remaining as the rump of the Papal States with Pope Pius IX tenuously holding on to power. Severn proved himself an able diplomat, his knowledge of the Italian language and people and his affability helping to mediate on touchy matters between the papal regime and the British government.

On many occasions he also advised and offered protection to Brits, whether tourists or expatriates, who found themselves in difficulties. He enjoyed meeting celebrated British visitors to Rome, such as the poets Elizabeth Barrett and Robert Browning, who had famously eloped and set up home in Florence; the couple were intrigued to hear Severn's memories of nursing the dying Keats. The Brownings spent several months in Rome in 1860–1, but sadly, Elizabeth was already seriously ill and died shortly after returning to Florence.

Severn retired as consul in 1872 and died in Rome seven years later at the age of 85, when he joined his old companion John Keats in the Protestant Cemetery.

Three of his seven children became noted artists themselves – his sons Walter and Arthur Severn, and most successfully, his daughter Ann Mary Newton, a talented portraitist whose patrons included Queen Victoria. Not a bad legacy.

The deeply touching portrait Severn drew of Keats as he lay on his deathbed now hangs in the Keats-Shelley House. Underneath it, Severn scrawled: '28 January, 1821, 3 o'clock morning, drawn to keep me awake. A deadly sweat was on him all this night.' Whatever else he did in his long and fruitful life, Joseph Severn is likely to be remembered most for the selfless, loving care he gave one of England's finest poets at the end of his days.

Russian souls

Throughout the nineteenth century, writers and artists were drawn inescapably to Italy, just as Byron and Shelley before them, inspired by its beauty, rich culture and history. One of them was the Ukrainian-born Russian novelist Nikolai Gogol, on whom Rome exerted the greatest pull. He lived in the city for much of the twelve years from 1836 to 1848, but even before then Italy had fired his imagination: he wrote his poem 'Ode to Italy' as early as 1829, when he was 20. The novel he considered his masterpiece, *Dead Souls* (1842), was written not only in Rome but mostly at the Caffè Greco, where Gogol, living on a parallel street, spent hours every day. He had left Russia because he felt better able to write about the country while outside its borders. 'I can write about Russia only in Rome, only there does it appear to me in all its scale and enormity,' Gogol wrote in a letter to a friend.

He had a number of like-minded Russian companions in Rome at the time – the artists Alexander Ivanov, Orest Kiprensky and Karl Bryullov, who lived on art scholarships and stipends and would congregate at the Greco. Gogol famously had a favourite table in the café where he'd often spend the entire day, the waiters remarking how he didn't appear to notice that morning had turned into nightfall. Hanging near that table today is a miniature portrait of Gogol, painted by the Russian artist Pavel Svedomsky.

Dead Souls chronicles the adventures of Pavel Ivanovich Chichikov, a middle-aged civil servant who plans to elevate his position in society by acquiring a large number of 'dead souls', i.e. serfs who are listed on the census of a landowner's estate though they have already died. Landowners have to pay taxes on their serfs, even the dead ones, until the names of the deceased are removed at the next census. Realising that as long as no one knows these serfs are dead, owning many of them will increase his prestige, Chichikov offers to take the dead souls off the landowners' hands and assume the tax burden.

Russian novelist Nikolai Gogol, sitting far left, at his favourite table at the Antico Caffè Greco in Rome.

The book satirised political corruption in tsarist Russia, but was nonetheless much enjoyed by Tsar Nicholas I, a fan of Gogol's work. It established Gogol's reputation as not only one of Russia's greatest novelists, but as an international literary giant. He was also recognised as the first Russian-language writer of the realist, or 'Natural School' of literature.

Thackeray enjoys a hot toddy

William Makepeace Thackeray took his teenage daughters Anny and Minny to Rome for Christmas 1853, and settled in for a lengthy stay at a palatial apartment on the Via della Croce. Only two streets away from the Via dei Condotti, it was well within the radius of the 'English ghetto'. Thackeray had good reason to visit the city then as he was writing his novel *The Newcomes: Memoirs of a Most Respectable Family*, and as part of it was set in Rome, he planned to carry out research. In the book, the character of Clive Newcome, an aspiring young painter, travels to Rome to study art and engross himself in the city's famed artists' colony. Thackeray aimed to soak up the ambience of that colony in order to portray it as accurately as possible.

A watercolour by the Austrian painter Ludwig Passini from the same period, titled *Artists at Café Greco in Rome*, shows a company of the top-hatted gents sitting and chatting around a small table, walking canes and pet dogs to hand. Many of these artists used the café as their postal address (not unlike London's coffee house habitués of two centuries earlier) and one of them can be seen standing by the counter, checking for any letters addressed to him.

Thackeray was doubtless aware of the Greco's reputation as the artists' chief hangout, and it figured prominently on his agenda:

> After dinner we go and have coffee and *mezzo-caldo* [hot toddy] at the Caffè Greco over the way. *Mezzo-caldo* is not a bad drink – a little rum – a slice of fresh citron – lots of pounded sugar, and boiling water for the rest. Here in various parts of the cavern (it is a vaulted low place) the various nations have their assigned quarters, and we drink our coffee and strong waters, and abuse Guido, or Rubens, or Bernini … and blow such a cloud of smoke as would make Warrington's lungs dilate with pleasure. We get very good cigars for a *bajoccho* and half – that is very good for us, cheap tobaccanalians.

A similarly colourful picture of the café was recorded a little earlier by William Mitchell Gillespie, an American engineer and author, in his book *Rome: As Seen by a New-Yorker in 1843–4*:

> The Caffé Greco is the general rendezvous of the artists of all nations … When you enter, you find the smoke so dense that you can scarcely see across the room, but through it dimly appear the long beards, fierce moustaches, slouched hats, slashed velvet jackets, frogged coats, and wild but intellectual countenances, which characterize most of the young artists of Rome.

As for Thackeray, he planned to carry on writing his book about the Newcomes while in Rome but fate was no help to him. He caught malaria, his fever came and went, and there were days when he wasn't well enough to work. As he had brought no governess along on the trip, he was also responsible for entertaining his daughters. Fortunately, he had genial and obliging company in Rome. The Barratts (Elizabeth and Robert) were there with their 4-year-old son Pen, as well as the prominent actress Fanny Kemble. All were very kind to Anny and Minny, and the Brownings introduced Thackeray to their good friend, the American sculptor William Wetmore Story, who lived in Rome with his wife and daughter Edith, aged 9.

As it happened, Edith too was ill, and Thackeray began visiting the child almost daily, each time reading to her the latest chapter of a fantastical children's story he was writing (and illustrating) to help her through her convalescence. Set in a fictional country, the plot revolved around the fortunes of four royal cousins and was a playful satire on the attitudes of royalty and the upper echelons of society. Edith never forgot the sickbed visits and storytelling of the writer whose 'large powerful frame' was 'dominated by his great head'. Half a century later, she recalled that 'it was a black day when the dear giant did not come'.

Published at Christmas 1854 as *The Rose and the Ring*, Thackeray's children's book was enthusiastically received. And Edith? When she grew up, she married into the House of Medici, the illustrious Florentine banking and political dynasty. She became the Marchesa Peruzzi di Medici, thereby slotting straight into the upper echelons of Thackeray's satire.

As the century wore on the neighbourhood of the Piazza di Spagna reinforced its position as the centre of gravity for Rome's Anglo-American community. It had English-language bookstores, an English bakery, banks catering to Anglophone clients and of course there was Babington's Tea Rooms, on the opposite side of the Spanish Steps from Keats's former home. It was opened in 1893 by two genteel young ladies: Isabel Cargill, from New Zealand, and Anna Maria Babington, a descendant of the Anthony Babington convicted in 1586 of plotting to assassinate Queen Elizabeth I in a conspiracy with Mary, Queen of Scots. As per usual, he was hanged, drawn and quartered – a riveting backstory, no doubt adding to the piquancy of the place as the expats sipped their tea. Nearby there was a scattering of English and American churches too, the closest being All Saints, an Anglican church a short walk away on the Via del Babuino. Meanwhile, for those who were just visiting there was the fashionable Hotel d'Inghilterra – the Hotel of England – in a handsome sixteenth-century building around the corner from the Via dei Condotti. The church, the hotel, and Babington's – now run by the fourth generation of the Cargill family and as resolutely English as ever – are all still there.

Artists of the open air

Rome and the Caffè Greco's significance as a focal point for artists, both foreign and Italian, continued. William Richmond – English painter, sculptor and designer, a member of the Arts and Crafts movement and best known for his decorative mosaics in St Paul's Cathedral – spent four years studying art in Rome during the 1860s and wrote about the café:

> Everyone who knows Rome has heard of the Caffè Greco, that haunt of Bohemia, the meeting-place of all nationalities, where every European language was heard from sundown to midnight. Writers, musicians,

painters, and sculptors, poor and rich, successful or only hopeful, turned in there after their supper or no supper to take the inevitable cup of coffee and smoke the inevitable pipe. The series of low-arched rooms leading one into another were filled with clouds of tobacco smoke as thick as a London fog. The clatter of cups, the chaos of languages – German, Russian, French, Spanish, even the Polish, Swedish, Norwegian, Greek and Balkan States were represented in this inclusive gathering of artists. Rome was indeed a centre of the world, it was more than that, it was the centre of Art, and the Caffè Greco was the centre of Rome even more than the Vatican.

Artists at Rome's Antico Caffè Greco, painting by Ludwig Passini, 1856.

While in Rome Richmond befriended the Pre-Raphaelite artist Frederick Leighton, the American artist Elihu Vedder (a long-term resident of Rome), and the Italian landscape painter Nino Costa, a fervent patriot who had fought under Garibaldi years earlier during the *Risorgimento* wars. The four were to influence and stimulate each other. When not seated around a table at the Greco, discussing their work and critiquing the artistic styles of the day, they went on painting excursions together to the countryside of the surrounding Roman Campagna.

During the later decades of the nineteenth century, Italian art was strongly influenced by the Pre-Raphaelite movement in Britain and the work of its chief proponents, William Holman Hunt, Edward Burne-Jones, John Everett Millais and Dante Gabriel Rossetti. They had banded together in reaction against what they regarded as the stilted styles and historical subjects favoured by the Royal Academy of Arts. Nino Costa, having been introduced to British art by his friend Frederick Leighton, was inspired to start an artistic movement of his own and in 1886, together with fellow Italian painter Giulio Aristide Sartorio, he founded In Arte Libertas – Latin for 'freedom in art'. The society aimed to promote Pre-Raphaelite art in Italy and that year held its first annual exhibition of works by Pre-Raphaelite artists, including Rossetti.

But the movement was about more than that. The members of In Arte Libertas enjoyed complete freedom of artistic expression and were encouraged to use whichever techniques and materials they preferred. They favoured painting from life and, rather than working in a studio, painted outdoors in the countryside, taking inspiration from nature. As for commercialised art, made with the sole purpose of profit and lacking any deeper spiritual meaning, they blatantly rejected it.

Naturally, the members of the movement held their gatherings at the Caffè Greco. Amongst the Italian artists involved was Enrico Coleman, Rome-born but of British nationality, son of the English painter Charles Coleman. Enrico was a successful painter in both oils and watercolours of the Campagna Romana landscapes. (Curiously, though he kept his British nationality throughout his life, he never once set foot in Britain.) Soon the members of In Arte Libertas had attracted a poet to their ranks – Gabriele d'Annunzio, who was looking for artists to illustrate his latest poetry collection: *Isaotta Guttadàuro ed altre poesi*. Coleman was one of nine who contributed artwork to the book, published in Rome in 1886. Two years later, a large group of In Arte Libertas artists were represented at the Italian Exhibition at Earl's Court, London.

On the death of Nino Costa in 1903, the movement was dissolved. However, the following year most of the members joined a new assemblage calling itself the XXV of the Roman Countryside (XXV because there were twenty-five of them). They still met up at the Greco, except for Sundays, when the nature lovers all boarded a train for the countryside, armed with canvases and easels, palettes and paintbrushes. There they happily painted away, and the day ended at a local tavern where they dined and imbibed the region's Frascati wine. They showed each other their day's work and the artist deemed to have created the most beautiful painting had their meal and the cost of the journey paid for by the others. In 1930, the XXV was dissolved by Mussolini's fascist regime.

An American in Rome

Of the expat artists and writers in Rome during the nineteenth century, Elihu Vedder was a link between the earlier period of the Romantic poets and the later community. The New York-born artist and poet had a long life, dying in Rome at the age of 86. Meeting Joseph Severn sometime in the 1860s or 1870s, he later wrote:

> I have since regretted that I did not realise how much of interest I might have collected from him of the days of Shelley, Keats and Byron … my friends George Simmonds and Charley Coleman installed themselves in the Keats apartment, and we revelled I fear somewhat regardless of the poet's memory – for we were desperately enamoured of our own lively lives just then …

Today, Vedder is best known for his fifty-five drawings for Edward FitzGerald's translation from the Persian of *The Rubáiyát of Omar Khayyám* – the deluxe edition published in Boston in 1884 – at the time one of the most influential illustrated books ever produced.

Few details were known about Vedder's daily doings in Rome, apart from what was contained in the random autobiographical sketches he produced late in life, but here the Caffè Greco had one last card to play. Several decades after his death a rich cache of 'Vedderiana' was discovered in old trunks in a storeroom above the café – photographs, drawings, letters, diaries and notebooks, material pertaining not only to Vedder but to his wide circle of English and American artist friends. It enabled the art historian Regina Soria to write her in-depth biography, *Elihu Vedder: American Visionary Artist in Rome*.

A new and absorbing pursuit

Artists, sculptors, poets, writers … One further band of innovators in the mid-nineteenth century chose the Caffè Greco as its informal headquarters: the early Italian photographers. In his article 'Photography in Rome' in the May 1852 issue of *The Art Journal*, Britain's most important nineteenth-century art magazine, Richard W. Thomas writes:

> In the first place a word about Roman photographers. I need hardly say that their places of rendezvous are the Lepre [a popular trattoria] and the Caffè Greco … I would recommend anyone visiting Rome with the intention of following this absorbing pursuit repair at once to the Caffè Greco.

Antico Caffè Greco in Rome, late nineteenth-century photograph.

Antico Caffè Greco in recent times.

The community of Rome-based photographers at the Greco included several important figures who became well known throughout Europe for their early success with paper negatives. They included the Italian landscape painter Giacomo Caneva, the French sculptor and medallist Frédéric Flachéron, the painter Eugène Constant, the architect Alfred-Nicolas Normand, the English artist James Anderson and the Scottish painter Robert Turnbull Macpherson. This international artistic set, known as the Roman School of Photography, was also called the Circle of the Caffè Greco. They encouraged new technical and aesthetic developments in the emerging medium and some gave photography lessons to the city's young enthusiasts.

Macpherson, with his red hair, Scottish brogue and kilt, stood out from the others. He was celebrated for the exceptional photographs he made using albumen on glass negatives, considered among the finest in Rome, and was the first photographer permitted to take pictures inside the Vatican. After his death in 1872, his obituary in *The Scotsman* stated that he was 'the father of photography in the Eternal City'.

The Via dei Condotti today is lined with high-end retail outlets. It boasts a Gucci, a Cartier, a Prada, a Louis Vuitton, an Armani, an Hermès, a Ferragamo, a Montblanc, a Jimmy Choo. In line with its ritzy neighbours, the Caffè Greco has become more exclusive too – it is no cheap option as a refreshment stop.

I often wonder what the great cultural figures of the past – Thackeray and Gogol, for instance – would make of our materialistic, consumption-mad twenty-first century. Their predictably scathing views might well make us squirm.

Chapter Seven

CAFÉ CENTRAL, VIENNA

Fast-forwarding to our own times, the Italians are rightly famous for the quality of their coffees and Parisian café life is justifiably renowned, but it is 'Viennese Coffee House Culture' which is listed by UNESCO as an Intangible Cultural Heritage, because the coffee house actually *created* Vienna's lifestyle and remains its most instantly recognisable cultural characteristic.

There is a fascinating story about how coffee arrived in Vienna and the city's first coffee house was opened. Naturally, it's to do with the Turks. Having destroyed the last vestiges of the Eastern Roman Empire at Constantinople in 1453, the Ottomans rampaged further westwards into Europe and in the sixteenth century, under Sultan Suleiman the Magnificent, managed to invade and annex the Kingdom of Hungary. They were to occupy it for a century and a half. But the Sultan didn't plan to stop there, hoping to take the greater prize of Vienna, capital of the Holy Roman Empire. In 1529, the Ottomans laid siege to the city, but fortunately for Christendom, the walls held and they were successfully rebuffed.

The Ottomans had a second go in the summer of 1683, unleashing a siege by a 170,000-strong army led by the Grand Vizier Kara Mustafa Pasha. The Habsburg monarchy had agreed a military union with the King of Poland, Jan III Sobieski, in order to repulse the Ottomans, but several weeks into the siege the Polish relief army had yet to arrive. Meanwhile the city was in the charge of military governor Count von Starhemberg, the Holy Roman Emperor Leopold I having already fled. With Vienna cut off and running out of supplies, and the woefully outnumbered and exhausted Viennese garrison on its last legs, von Starhemberg called for a volunteer to slip through the Turkish lines and reach the imperial forces under Charles V, Duke of Lorraine, camped a few miles away across the Danube, to request urgent help. Step forward a Polish trader, translator and soldier called Jerzy Franciszek Kulczycki. An extraordinary linguist – besides Polish and German he spoke fluent Hungarian, Serbian, Romanian and Turkish – he volunteered to leave starving Vienna and inform the duke of their desperate plight.

Kulczycki, who had spent many years living and working amongst the Turks and knew their customs, departed the city wearing Turkish attire, accompanied by a similarly disguised servant. He hoodwinked his way through the enemy encampment, singing Ottoman songs and gathering useful intelligence. After contacting the duke, he made it back to Vienna once more through the Turkish

Jerzy Franciszek Kulczycki, now the celebrated Georg Franz Kolschitzky, dressed in Turkish gear.

tents and artillery emplacements, and relayed the news that relief was imminent. With morale thus boosted, the city council resolved not to surrender but to fight on. Within days, Jan Sobieski's Polish army arrived, joined the duke's imperial troops, and lifted the two-month-long siege. The great Battle of Vienna on 12 September (featuring the largest cavalry charge in history) saw the Ottomans comprehensively trounced. It was a turning point in the centuries-old conflict between the Habsburgs and the Ottomans. Christian Europe was saved and the Turks began the Great Retreat, which saw them driven out of Hungary and Eastern Europe.

Kulczycki was hailed a folk hero by the grateful Viennese. The city council awarded him a house, as well as a considerable sum of money. And there was something else. When the defeated Turks fled their camp they left behind thousands of tents, oxen and camels, 9,000 carts filled with supplies and weapons, a vast stash of money and

Jerzy Franciszek Kulczycki at his Blue Bottle Coffee House in Vienna, celebrating his role in repelling the Ottoman Turks.

gold, and hundreds of sacks of coffee beans. The spoils of war were distributed, but no one knew what to do with the strange beans. Well, nobody except for Kulczycki, who was of course familiar with the custom of making and drinking coffee. He was allowed to keep the sacks and before long had established the first street stall introducing Turkish coffee to the denizens of Vienna. Then in 1686, he opened a coffee house in the city called the Blue Bottle. Apparently a popular proprietor, he addressed his customers as *bruderherz* (brother-heart) and no doubt regaled them with embroidered tales of his heroics during the perilous days of the siege.

This is the oft-told tale of how Vienna's history with coffee began, and the Viennese are sticking to it. The name Jerzy Franciszek Kulczycki was duly Germanised to Georg Franz Kolschitzky and his statue continues to stand proudly on his namesake street, Kolschitzkygasse. Some of Vienna's cafés still display his portrait in the window, generally dressed as a Turk. He is an icon of Viennese café society.

Further research suggests that the Blue Bottle might not have been the city's first coffee house after all. It seems an Armenian merchant named Johannes Diodato, born in Constantinople, opened one a year earlier. Like Kulczycki, he had learnt all about coffee making from the Turks and as a trader had access to the beans. His coffee house was a simple affair in his own apartment, where customers sat on wooden benches. But according to some sources, Diodato was actually a secret agent working for the imperial court, and his little set-up was a useful cover for a meeting place where spies passed on secret messages – good cloak-and-dagger stuff. Diodato scarpered from Vienna some years later, so it was said, after being involved in one act of espionage too many …

With the Treaty of Carlowitz in 1699, the Austrians and their would-be conquerors, the Turks, ended their mutual enmity. By 1719, relations between the former adversaries was positively rosy. In that year, the Turkish ambassador was invited to view the ongoing construction of Prince Eugene of Savoy's Belvedere palace complex in Vienna, along with its splendid gardens. As reported in the *Wienerisches Diarium* newspaper, after seeing 'the stately buildings, the rare plants and animals, the pools and water wonders [fountains]', the high-ranking Turk was 'regaled with confections, fruits, coffee and lemonade'. Was he aware that the Viennese and their Royals had taken up the Turkish custom of coffee drinking courtesy of a crafty anti-Ottoman spy?

A golden compromise

In the latter part of the nineteenth century, the coffee houses of Vienna became focal points for intellectual ferment, plots and intrigues, discoveries and emerging cultural movements.

This was their golden era. Following major political reforms, Emperor Franz Joseph of the House of Habsburg united the Austrian Empire and the Kingdom of

Hungary in a dual monarchy through the so-called Compromise of 1867. Austria and Hungary thus became equal powers in a multi-national empire with a population nearing 50 million. It encompassed a dozen ethnic groups – Germans, Hungarians, Poles, Czechs, Ukrainians, Slovaks, Slovenes, Croatians, Serbs, Bosnians, Italians and Romanians – speaking fifteen different languages. To be an officer in the Austro-Hungarian Army you had to be able to give commands in eleven languages besides German.

Vienna was now a thriving cosmopolitan capital, attracting newcomers from the empire's far-flung regions, and a growing number of coffee houses sprang up to appeal to them. They were comfortable, congenial and inexpensive places where you could sit for as long as you liked, sip *kaffee* and eat *apfelstrudel*, read the papers, meet friends and colleagues, play chess or cards, discuss matters both important and frivolous, or write your next article, poem, play or novel.

The Compromise also emancipated the Jews, granting them equal rights under the law, and by the end of the nineteenth century there were some 2 million of them living in the empire. Vienna had one of the largest Jewish communities and it played a fundamental role in the city's café life, as Jews were both passionate café habitués and, indeed, the proprietors of many. (Its twin capital of Budapest likewise had a large and thriving Jewish population, so much so that anti-Semites mockingly called it 'Judapest'.)

Viennese style

A recognisable style of Viennese coffee house décor emerged. They had high ceilings and tall windows, were furnished with marble-topped tables and bentwood chairs, and lit with chandeliers. There would be a long table with a row of newspapers attached to wooden holders, and often billiard tables too. When you ordered your coffee – either 'brown' (with milk) or black – a formally dressed waiter would bring it on a little silver tray with a complimentary glass of cold tap water. Some cafés even brought you a colour chart from which you could choose the precise hue of coffee you fancied.

By the late nineteenth century, coffee houses were no longer the exclusive domain of men. Women and even families spent time in them too, if not as much as the male intellectuals and creative types for whom the coffee house, given the long hours they spent there, was in a sense their real 'home'. And this same style of coffee house now flourished in the empire's other major cities – Budapest, Prague, Krakow, Zagreb, Trieste.

Enter (and exit) Stefan Zweig

One of the best depictions of Vienna's coffee house scene during the heady days of the Austro-Hungarian Empire came from the Viennese novelist Stefan Zweig. He spent the Second World War in exile, having fled the Nazis, and in his final

The Café Central in Vienna, late nineteenth century.

Vienna's Café Central, engraving by Kupferstich von Kollarz, 1881

book – a memoir called *The World of Yesterday* – he looked back wistfully on his life as a young man:

> Our finest place of education for everything new was the coffee house. To understand this, one has to know that the Viennese café is an institution of a special kind which is not comparable to any other in the world. It is actually a kind of democratic club, accessible to anyone for an inexpensive cup of coffee … all Viennese papers were available and not only the Viennese ones but those of the entire German empire, as well as the French and English and Italian and American ones, in addition to the important literary and art magazines of the world. Thus we knew everything that went on first-hand, we knew of every book that appeared, of every performance no matter where it took place … Nothing perhaps has contributed as much to the intellectual agility and international orientation of the Austrian as the fact that he could exhaustively find out in the coffee house about all the activities in the world

> and discuss them at the same time in the circle of his friends. We sat there daily for hours, nothing escaped us.

Perhaps his losses were more than he could bear. Along with his wife Lotte, Zweig committed suicide in Brazil in 1942, shortly before the book was published.

To the Coffee House!

The most famous of all Viennese cafés is the Café Central, opened in 1876 and located in the city centre, as its name implies. When you enter the lush interior with its ornate vaulted ceiling and marble pillars, you'll be greeted by the life-sized papier mâché figure of a somewhat glum-looking, balding man with a bushy moustache, seated at one of the small round tables. This is Peter Altenberg, the Austrian writer and poet who, more than anyone, was the embodiment of Vienna's flourishing coffee house scene during the Austro-Hungarian Empire. An arch-bohemian, he was known as the patron saint of the Central because he practically lived there. It was even given as his address on his calling card, so it was where his post was delivered. He once quipped that the best thing about being in a coffee house was that you're neither at home nor out in the fresh air. (Well, a poet's home was likely to be cramped and cheerless, and which genial man of letters would prefer the great outdoors to a welcoming interior peopled with his chosen companions?)

Altenberg had a reputation for boozing, drug taking and womanising, and was a depressive who spent time in mental institutions. Always short of cash, he was good at making friends and acquiring benefactors, and could charm people into paying for his meals, drinks and even the rent at his cheap lodgings. Cigarettes, meanwhile, he cadged from the café's waiters. Yet he was a talented writer who described himself as 'a little pocket mirror' reflecting the world around him, and was a virtuoso of the closely observed short story about the people and events of everyday life. His first published collection in 1896, *Wie Ich es Sehe* (*How I See It*), set him on his way, and he had some distinguished champions. Initially discovered by the Austrian dramatist Arthur Schnitzler, he was later applauded by the writer Karl Kraus, himself a three-time nominee for the Nobel Prize in Literature. Thomas Mann said that reading Altenberg was 'love at first sound'. And Franz Kafka (who visited the Café Central when in Vienna) remarked that Altenberg had a talent for 'finding the splendours of the world like cigarette butts in the ashtrays of coffee houses'.

As well as being a captivating, eccentric personality, Altenberg was a key member of the Jung-Wien (Young Vienna) movement, composed of late nineteenth-century writers who met first at the Café Griensteidl, and after its demolition in 1897, relocated to the Café Central. They eschewed the literary naturalism of the time, regarding it as outdated, and experimented with new forms such as Symbolism and Impressionism. They challenged too the straitlaced Victorian attitudes which pervaded the era's literature, in favour of societal truths and emotional and sexual honesty. What they wanted was an art reflecting the emerging industrial world with its new technologies and urbanisation, and Altenberg was an influential member of the movement.

He was also a contradictory character who championed the rights of workers and displayed an unusual degree of empathy for women and children, servants and all manner of underdogs. Yet he wasn't above taking advantage of the much younger lasses who caught his eye, and when one of them protested that he only wanted her for sex, he replied: 'What's so *only* about that?'

His feelings about his beloved Café Central were summed up in his poem entitled 'To the Coffee House!'

> When you are worried, have trouble of one sort or another – to the coffee house!
> When she did not keep her appointment, for one reason or other – to the coffee house!
> When your shoes are torn and dilapidated – coffee house!
> When your income is four hundred crowns and you spend five hundred – coffee house!

And a little further on:

> You could not find a mate to suit you – coffee house!
> You feel like committing suicide – coffee house!
> You hate and despise human beings, and at the same time you cannot be happy without them – coffee house!

It continues in this vein for several more lines.

As Peter Altenberg observed life from his table at the Café Central, the pioneering psychoanalyst Sigmund Freud was not far away, taking refreshment at *his* favourite hangout, the elegant Café Landtmann. Freud was often to be seen there, cogitating on his theories and therapies, or in intense discussion with medical friends and colleagues. One such was Alfred Adler (with whom he later fell out), the founder of the school of 'individual psychology', a theory of human behaviour predicated on the principle that each individual has a unique personality.

Freud's radical new field of psychoanalysis was attracting serious attention in Vienna by the 1890s. Altenberg himself had been analysed by a psychiatrist and diagnosed with 'over-excitation of the nervous system', leading to 'an incapacity for gainful employment'. This analysis suited him just fine – it meant he could carry on with his freewheeling bohemian ways. He later mocked his shrink as a pompous bore in a story called *Sanatorium for the Mentally Imbalanced.*

Peter Altenberg at Vienna's Café Central, 1907 photograph.

Another prominent Viennese writer of the time, columnist and theatre critic Alfred Polgar, was so deeply ensconced at the Café Central that he wrote an essay extolling the distinctive virtues of the place, called 'Theory of the Café Central'. It was, he claimed, unlike any other coffee house:

> Its inhabitants are, for the most part, people whose hatred of their fellow human beings is as fierce as their longing for people, who want to be alone but need companionship for it. … their quivering solo voices cannot do without the support of the chorus. … There are writers, for example, who are unable to carry out their literary chores anywhere but at the Café Central. Only there, only at the tables of idleness, is the worktable laid for them, only there, enveloped by the air of indolence, will their inertia become fecundity.

A Zionist rejects café society

Zweig, Altenberg, Schnitzler, Kraus, Kafka, Freud, Adler, Polgar – all Jewish intellectuals heartily embedded in the Austro-Hungarian Empire's *fin-de-siècle* coffee house culture. But also in Vienna at this time, and a Café Central regular, was a Jewish thinker prepared to take a radically different stance. Theodor Herzl was born in Budapest, son of a wealthy businessman. In 1878, when he was 18, the family moved to Vienna and Theodor studied law at Vienna University. But he soon turned from the law to journalism, penning articles for the Viennese paper *Neue Freie Presse,* alongside writing plays for the Viennese stage.

Herzl had believed in the importance of secular Jews such as himself becoming wholly assimilated into Central European civilisation and culture, to shake off their long history of being ostracised and oppressed. However, towards the end of the nineteenth century he was losing confidence in this belief. The Austrian politician Karl Lueger, a zealous Catholic and anti-Semitic demagogue, rose to prominence in 1895 and two years later was elected mayor of Vienna. He pressed for discriminatory policies against the empire's non-German speakers and a restriction on immigration of Jews from the eastern regions. In *The History of Anti-Semitism*, French historian Léon Poliakov writes: 'It soon became apparent that especially in Vienna any political group that wanted to appeal to the artisans had no chance of success without an anti-Semitic platform … Lueger raised the banner of anti-Semitism.'

Many people, including many Jews, contended that Lueger's anti-Semitic rhetoric was hollow – merely a tactic to win popular support – and that he was basically a decent sort with numerous Jewish friends. Stefan Zweig, a young man in Vienna during Lueger's term in office, later recalled his administration as having been 'perfectly just and democratic'.

But Herzl, convinced the anti-Semitism was all too real and couldn't be defeated or ignored, felt compelled to reject his earlier faith in Jewish emancipation and integration into European society. Perhaps a better solution for Jews was to remove themselves from Europe and establish a homeland of their own. His pamphlet, *Der Judenstaat* (*The Jewish State*), powerfully advocated the creation of an independent Jewish nation, whilst his play, *The New Ghetto*, aimed to show the lack of true equality for Jews in Vienna. Its protagonist is a Jewish lawyer unable to break through the 'social ghetto' in which the city's Jews are confined, no matter how

Café Central in Vienna, at the turn of the twentieth century.

assimilated they think they are. Herzl's writings were influential in the formation of the Zionist movement and he became its leader.

In his earlier days, Herzl had been as keen a café-goer as anyone, but once he became an ardent Zionist, he saw Vienna's café society in a different light. His 1902 novel *Altneuland* (*The Old New Land*) is his utopian vision for a thriving, cosmopolitan Jewish homeland in Palestine. But its first chapter is set in 'one of the most charming of Viennese cafés' where the protagonist, 23-year-old Friedrich Löewenberg – a customer since his student days, attending every afternoon 'with bureaucratic punctuality' – is sitting alone at a marble table, sunk in melancholy. He'd been carefree once, but now only his dreams are left. He drinks coffee, reads the papers and looks around at the other young middle-class Jewish men there as they idle their time away playing billiards. Over-educated and under-employed, 'they could not, like their Christian colleagues, slip into public posts'. Their lives are going nowhere. Herzl is laying the ground for his novel's message: the coffee houses of Europe are not where Jews can ever truly belong. They need to build a new society elsewhere – preferably in the Land of Israel, where their tribe had its origin.

Theodor Herzl died at the age of 44, only two years after his book was published and several decades before his vision came to fruition. He was buried in Vienna but in 1949, the year after the founding of the State of Israel, his remains were brought to Jerusalem and reburied on the site named after him, Mount Herzl.

Communist firebrands

In the early twentieth century, Vienna had a population of 1.7 million and was the largest city in Europe after London, Paris and Berlin. It was also a cauldron of political tensions – a conflict between nationalist and socialist ideas – and the simmering ethnic rivalries within the empire were about to come to a head. In these years leading up to the outbreak of the First World War, Vienna was home, for longer or shorter periods, to an astonishing array of figures who went on to change the course of history.

Leon Trotsky (then still known by his birth surname of Bronstein) fled tsarist Russia after the attempted revolution of 1905 was crushed, and in 1907 settled in Vienna to work as a journalist. He was fond of the city, preferring it to other European capitals such as London, where he had lived earlier. The Central European ambience, the *Gemütlichkeit* – cosy geniality – of its cafés was something Trotsky loved and he became a well-known figure at the Central. He developed cordial relations with many of its writers, especially Peter Altenberg and Karl Kraus. He enjoyed playing chess with Alfred Polgar and by all accounts, the pair were formidable opponents.

Of course, he also had a number of Marxist and Bolshevik-leaning friends in the city, it was a hub for political émigrés from Russia. With its large population of industrial workers and its suburbs packed with smoke-belching factories, Vienna was regarded by left-wing radicals as a vital centre for their revolutionary struggle. From 1908, Trotsky edited the newspaper *Pravda*, which had moved its base there. For a while, editorial control of the paper was fought over by the Bolsheviks and more moderate Mensheviks – a tussle from which Trotsky tried to distance himself. Meanwhile he gave the paper a tabloid format, making it more easily readable, and it gained many readers among the Russian working class.

One of Trotsky's closest associates in Vienna was the wealthy Adolph Joffe, a

Trotsky reading his paper, *Pravda*, in Vienna, *c.*1910.

militant member of the Russian Social Democratic Workers' Party, who helped him edit *Pravda* and even used his family's money to prop up the financially strapped paper. Joffe was in Vienna studying psychoanalysis under Freud's rival, Alfred Adler, and proceeded to introduce Trotsky to this burgeoning medical field. Trotsky got to know Adler well and retained a lifelong fascination with psychoanalysis, believing, curiously, that it had a lot in common with Marxism – perhaps because both are concerned with the interrelation between the individual and society.

In January 1913, Joseph Stalin was sent to Vienna by Lenin (then living in exile in Krakow and hanging out at the fashionable Café Noworolski), in order to research the article to be called 'Marxism and the National Question'. Its purpose was to analyse the ways in which Marxism could be applied in a multi-ethnic empire such as Austria-Hungary, and by extension to the multi-ethnic Russian Empire. It wasn't the easiest task for Stalin: he was supposed to interview Austrian Marxists and study German texts but could neither speak nor read the language. He lived at the house of a rich Bolshevik sympathiser, Alexander Troyanovsky, near the Habsburgs' summer residence, Schönbrunn Palace. But he spent a fair amount of time during his month's stay in Vienna with Trotsky, who took his fellow Bolshevik – whom he described as short and thin, 'his greyish-brown skin covered in pockmarks' – to the Café Central so he could take in the atmosphere and observe the regulars.

Despite the linguistic difficulties, Stalin finished his article and in February returned to Russia. Lenin was happy with the work of this 'wonderful Georgian' and the piece was published the following month under the name Stalin – the Russian word for 'steel' – a pseudonym recently adopted by the communist formerly known as Iosif Dzhugashvili. As the article established his reputation with the Bolshevik movement, he decided to stick permanently with this catchier name.

Someone else destined to make his mark in the communist world was living in Vienna during this period. Josip Broz was born in another part of the Austro-Hungarian Empire – the Croatian village of Kumrovec. From his late teens, he began moving around from city to city, doing a variety of jobs and getting involved in trade unionism and leftist politics. By the autumn of 1912, he was living with his older brother Martin in Vienna and got a job at a factory. Then Broz moved further south to Wiener Neustadt, where he worked as a machinist and occasional test driver for the Austro-Daimler car company (and perfected his dancing and fencing skills). But the following spring he was off again, having been conscripted into the Austro-Hungarian Army. It wasn't until the 1930s that Broz, by then a true communist firebrand, changed his name to Tito, by which he would become known the world over as the long-running leader of the former Yugoslavia.

A bum from the cafés of Vienna

In the midst of Vienna's assorted left-wing radicals was the down-at-heel artist, Adolf Hitler. He had arrived as an 18-year-old from Linz in 1907 to study at the

Academy of Fine Arts, but had been rejected twice. Hitler was earning a pittance selling his postcard illustrations of Vienna's imposing buildings, living at a homeless men's dormitory, listening to his beloved Wagner at the Opera House (though he could only afford the cheap standing room tickets), and lounging about in cafés. Sometimes these were of the humble working-class variety, but he had a penchant for more glamorous ones like the Central too. After all, in those days it cost very little to buy a coffee at a place like the Central or the Landtmann, no one moved you on when you'd finished it, and you could read all the newspapers for free.

Many years later, when he was Reich Chancellor, Hitler liked to reminisce about the time he'd spent as a young man in Vienna's cafés, describing them as 'a source of quietude, meditation and education'. Later still, after the Third Reich had come crashing down and Hitler was dead, Hermann Göring dismissed his erstwhile Führer as 'a bum from the cafés of Vienna'.

Was there a moment in early 1913 when, beneath the Central's vaulted ceiling, the wily Trotsky and Stalin sat together, a table or two away from the sullen Hitler – all three of them sipping a *kaffee* and musing on how they would like to upend the world order? Perhaps not. But there could have been …

The following year, with rumours swirling of an impending war, the Austrian politician Victor Adler warned Count Leopold Berchtold, Foreign Minister of Austria-Hungary, that a major war could provoke a communist revolution in Russia, to which Berchtold jokingly replied: 'And who would lead this revolution? Perhaps Mr Bronstein, sitting over there at Café Central?'

When that war did indeed break out, in which Austria-Hungary fought against the Russian Empire, Trotsky was forced to flee Vienna for neutral Switzerland to avoid arrest as a Russian émigré. Three years later, as Adler had predicted, came the Russian Revolution, with Trotsky as one of its leaders. Back at the Café Central, head waiter Josef was not surprised by the development. 'I always knew Herr Doktor Bronstein would go far in life,' he remarked, 'but I shouldn't have thought he'd leave without paying for the four mochas he owes me.'

Choosing your coffee

Nowadays the Café Central is listed as a must-see in the guidebooks, so you are liable to encounter a long line of tourists outside, patiently waiting to enter. If you want to bypass the queue and head straight in, either reserve a table in advance or arrive not much later than 9 a.m. Of course, the impecunious writers and artists of yesteryear would be shocked at the prices on the menus at their favourite cafés today; even well-heeled tourists are known to raise an eyebrow.

And a word on ordering coffee at Vienna's cafés. It can be confusing. There are so many types it makes the selection at Starbucks seem positively spartan. *Kleiner brauner*, *grosser brauner*, *kleiner schwarzer*, *grosser schwarzer*, *verlängerter*, *einspänner*, *kapuziner*, *mokka*, *Wiener melange*, *franziskaner*, *obermayer*, *kaffee verkehrt*, *kaffee mit schlagobers*, *häferlkaffee*. These variations are all to do with the quantity of coffee in your cup (or glass) and whether it's served black, with plain milk, frothed milk (*milchschaum*), single cream (*obers*) or whipped cream (*schlagobers*), and whether it has a little milk or a lot, a modest topping of cream or a hefty heap.

There are other distinctions too. The *überstürtzer*, for example, is an upside-down concoction in which whipped cream is put into an empty cup and a double espresso poured over it. The *obermayer* is a double portion of coffee into which very cold single cream is poured over the back of a spoon – invented by one Herbert Obermeier of the Viennese Philharmonic Orchestra, who always drank a coffee during intermissions and needed it cooled down quickly before the break was over.

There are also various alcoholic options, such as the Maria Theresa. In that regal indulgence – said to have been a preference of the Habsburg queen – coffee is mixed with a cheeky shot of orange liqueur.

Amidst this plethora of beverages, the brilliant Stefan Zweig himself would have been all at sea.

Stefan Zweig, the classic Austro-Hungarian café intellectual.

Chapter Eight

CAFÉ SPERL, VIENNA

There were hundreds of coffee houses in *fin-de-siècle* Vienna, and like their seventeenth-century counterparts in London, each became associated with a certain category of customer. Some were gathering places for businessmen, some for aristocrats, others for factory workers or students, still others for academics or chess players or middle-class ladies' circles. And as already seen, there were cafés linked with the literati, most notably the Central. The great composers too had their favoured haunts. In earlier times, Beethoven and Mozart frequented the Augarten Café, whilst Schubert preferred the Café Bogner, and Franz Lehár – composer of *The Merry Widow* and other operettas – was most often to be seen at the Café Museum.

Meanwhile, the Café Sperl – founded in 1880 on Gumpendorferstrasse, a little outside the inner city – was patronised by high-ranking army officers,

Café Sperl, in *fin-de-siècle* Vienna.

Inside Vienna's Café Sperl, late nineteenth century.

many connected to the nearby military academy. One regular customer was the hawkish General Conrad von Hötzendorf, the future Chief of Staff of the Austro-Hungarian Army. He would be the first to agitate for war against Serbia following the assassination in Sarajevo of Archduke Franz Ferdinand by the teenage Serb separatist Gavrilo Princip.

But it wasn't all military swagger around the tables at the Sperl. The café was even more closely associated with artists, in particular the Secessionists, whose radical artistic movement was to achieve such lasting international influence. From the mid-1890s, the Sperl was the customary meeting place of the Siebener Club (Club of Seven), a set of artists dissatisfied with Vienna's traditional, conservative artistic establishment, which had a stranglehold on the city's exhibition halls. They would exchange ideas on modern art and express their desire for an independent exhibition space open to newer artistic styles. As they sat and chatted, and drank coffee at their *Stammtisch*, or regulars' table, they were in the habit of drawing little caricatures on scraps of paper or even directly on to the marble tabletops. The group included Josef Hoffmann, Koloman Moser, Carl Moll and Fritz Warendorfer. And they were soon joined by the like-minded Gustav Klimt, already the recipient of the Emperor's Golden Order of Merit for his murals in Vienna's Burgtheater.

Their meetings at the Sperl resulted in their break with the official Association of Austrian Artists, and in 1897, they founded the Vienna Secession. By now the movement was forty-strong and included painters, graphic artists, designers,

Artists of the Vienna Secession, 1902, with Gustav Klimt at the back, second from left.

illustrators, sculptors and architects. Klimt was elected president. The Secession marked a definitive move away from the past and into a new era in which the arts and crafts were integrated, equal in importance and liberated from commercial constraints and conservative tastes. The Secessionists' motto was '*Der Zeit ihre Kunst, der Kunst ihre Freiheit*' (To every age its art, to every art its freedom). Art suddenly became a lot more sensual and suggestive, not to mention more sexually explicit.

The Vienna Secession was closely related to Germany's Jugendstil (Young-style) movement, a version of Art Nouveau, and also strongly influenced by Britain's Arts and Crafts movement, whose leading lights were the English textile designer William Morris and Scottish architect Charles Rennie Mackintosh.

Nudes of the sacred spring

The movement soon had its own mouthpiece, a monthly magazine called *Ver Sacrum* (Latin for 'sacred spring'), to which Klimt was a prolific contributor.

Its articles set out the movement's principles, for example: 'We want art that is not a slave to foreign influences but at the same time is neither afraid nor hateful of them,' and advocated a universal art that could be appreciated by everyone, poor and rich, powerful and powerless.

The magazine reproduced artwork by the movement's members, but this could lead to problems. One early issue was confiscated by the authorities because Klimt's pencil sketches of nudes 'violated the sense of shame with its depiction of nudity and thus created public outrage'. Klimt's response was that he refused to deal with 'boorish people'. He could afford to brush off the critics, as he was getting a lot of commissioned work from his private clients, members of the Viennese upper class. And besides, provoking indignation was part of his plan.

Because the work of the Secessionists was unwelcome at Vienna's prevailing exhibition halls, they evidently required a venue of their own where they could display it. To this end the architect Joseph Maria Olbrich, one of the Secession's founders, designed the grandiose Secession Building, opened in 1898. The domed edifice with its exotic, oriental influences was ridiculed by the movement's opponents, who dubbed it 'the Mausoleum' and 'the Crematorium'. But it was a triumph – the city's first gallery dedicated to contemporary art, a home not only for the work of the Viennese Secessionists but for avant-garde artists from all over Europe. Not least, it introduced the French Impressionist painters and sculptor August Rodin to the Viennese public.

Klimt produced his admired *Beethoven Frieze*, in honour of the composer, for the venue's fourteenth exhibition in 1902. The show attracted 57,000 visitors – including Klimt's supporter, Emperor Franz Joseph – and 218 works of art were sold.

The Secession later split into two different factions due to a disagreement over its future direction, and Klimt and several of his fellow artists resigned from it. Whilst the organisation carried on, it lost much of the innovative excitement of its earlier years.

A woman's fate

It would appear that all the progressive, imaginative artists of the Vienna Secession were men, but that isn't the case. There were a few women in the movement, but as per the values and attitudes of the time, they were deemed of lower rank. And whilst the men are still lauded today, the women have been largely ignored. The Russian-born painter and sculptress Elena Luksch-Makowsky is a case in point. She showed her work in important Secession exhibitions, an admittance doubtless made easier by her marriage to a Secession member, the Viennese sculptor Richard Luksch. Featuring prominently in the 1902 Beethoven exhibition, a year later she did the illustrations – a series of woodcuts – for a special issue of *Ver Sacrum*. But she had to function largely as an unofficial member of the Secession, without voting rights. In 1907 she and her husband moved to Germany and it was there that she worked on a sculpture called *Frauenschicksal* (*Woman's Fate*), depicting a distressed-looking woman with children at her feet. She must have sensed something about her own fate, because after she and Luksch divorced in 1921 she struggled to support their three sons on her own and remained financially insecure for the rest of her life.

Scandals and seductions

Despite the many other talents involved, male and female, the two most glittering stars of the Vienna Secession movement were undeniably Gustav Klimt and, in time, his young protégé, Egon Schiele.

In 1857, when Emperor Franz Joseph decided to dismantle the medieval walls surrounding Vienna – which two centuries earlier had protected the city during the Ottomans' siege – it freed up the whole area for new construction. The outcome was the creation of the magnificent boulevard known as the Ringstrasse, a ring road encircling the inner city, and the many impressive buildings lining it in a medley of architectural styles. The City Hall, symbol of a prosperous commercial metropolis, was built in the Northern European Gothic style; the Parliament was Neoclassical, in a nod to the origins of democracy in ancient Athens; the University of Vienna, with its focus on science and the humanities, was inspired by the Italian Renaissance; and the grandiose private palaces of the nobles and other wealthy citizens embraced an idealised blend of past architectural forms, known colloquially as 'Ringstrasse style'.

Klimt, whose artistic talent was recognised while he was still a teenage pupil at Vienna's Kunstgewerbeschule (Arts and Crafts School), first won renown for the murals he painted in some of the Ringstrasse's buildings. But his obsession with the erotic and his portrayals of naked women in seductive poses plunged him into scandals. His work represented a complete break with the way women were traditionally depicted in nineteenth-century paintings, as full-figured and motherly, domesticated and passive. Instead, his were lean, sexually confident, vampish. In many cases, breasts were uncovered, fig leaves whipped away from genitalia. Authorities that had commissioned his work later labelled him a pornographer. But their derision didn't stop Klimt from being Austrian high society's most sought-after portrait painter. He executed his pictures in an inimitable style, often incorporating shimmering gold leaf, as in his famous portrait of the socialite Adele Bloch-Bauer, thought to have been one of his mistresses.

Nor was his originality confined to his pictures. Klimt liked to work wearing sandals, a capacious floor-length smock, and no undergarments – a get-up that facilitated his dalliances with his models. He never married, but ended up fathering some fourteen children. Yet he somehow managed to be discreet about his private life, rarely revealing anything about himself to the public. 'There is nothing special about me,' he wrote. 'I am a painter who paints day after day from morning till night … Whoever wants to know something about me … should study my paintings.'

Gustav Klimt outside his studio in Vienna, 1912.

A generation younger, Egon Schiele was the son of a provincial railway stationmaster and his earliest childhood artistic efforts were drawings of the trains that rumbled past their house. His ill-tempered father reckoned he spent too much time drawing, and destroyed his sketchbooks; in due course, he contracted syphilis and went insane. In one fit of madness, Egon's papa set fire to all his railways stocks, so that when he finally died in 1905 his family became destitute. Aged 15, Egon fell under the guardianship of his uncle, a railway inspector. Disappointed that his ward didn't wish to follow in the family's footsteps and work on the railways, Egon's uncle nevertheless recognised the boy's artistic talent and grudgingly allowed him to study art. Schiele first gained a place at the School of Arts and Crafts, where Klimt had studied, and then, in 1907, enrolled at the more prestigious Academy of Fine Arts (the institution that was to reject Hitler the following year).

Schiele was heavily influenced by the work of Klimt and when the two met, they struck up an immediate friendship. Klimt began mentoring the then 17-year-old, and even modelled for him, but he probably couldn't have foreseen that his protégé's work would one day be regarded as even more shocking than his own.

There was a highly narcissistic element to Schiele's early work. He made many self-portraits in bizarre poses, with arms outstretched, crucifix-style, and with strangely splayed fingers. Along with Klimt, he even dared to depict the unmentionable practice of masturbation – not at all what conservative Austrian society was accustomed to. Among his favourite subjects were the young Viennese prostitutes, their nude figures often contorted and sexually charged.

For a few years he abandoned Vienna and lived in the provinces with his teenage lover, a red-haired model called Wally Neuzil, whom he had inherited from Klimt. Spotted painting a nude in his garden, he was kicked out of the first town, whilst in the second town he was arrested for allegedly seducing and kidnapping a minor. While he was in jail awaiting trial, his studio was raided by the police and a hundred or so drawings seized. The seduction and kidnapping charges were dropped, but he was convicted of the crime of 'public immorality' for exhibiting and distributing his 'obscene' drawings. The outraged judge even held one of the offending drawings above a candle and burnt it in court, as Schiele looked on with contempt. But as with Klimt, charges of pornography didn't put off the wealthy patrons and buyers of his work.

Schiele returned to Vienna in 1914. As war broke out, he split with Wally in order to marry a more respectable middle-class girl, Edith Harms. Schiele now became interested in the themes of motherhood and family; Edith became the model for most of his female figures and he painted her fully clothed. Drafted into the army, he spent part of his military service stationed at a POW camp where he was allowed to draw and paint imprisoned Russian soldiers. His commanding officer even let him have a disused storeroom to use as his studio.

By 1917, Schiele was once again back in Vienna. Fifty of his works were displayed prominently in the Secession's forty-ninth exhibition in 1918, and he designed the exhibition's advertising poster: inspired by Leonardo da Vinci's painting *The Last Supper*, it depicted himself in the place of Christ. The show was a great success, leading to higher prices for Schiele's work and a slew of new commissions.

Tragically, an era was about to come to an abrupt end. In February 1918 – shortly before the Secession exhibition – Klimt died aged 55 of a stroke and pneumonia, triggered by the Spanish Flu pandemic, which had reached Europe at the beginning of that year. A distraught Schiele sat by his old mentor's deathbed and made sketches of him, showing his face heavily lined, his hollowed eyes closed. That October, Schiele's wife Edith, six months pregnant, also contracted the Spanish Flu. He nursed her tenderly, but didn't stop working. His last drawing of her – titled *Edith Schiele on Her Deathbed* – poignantly captured her suffering. Stricken with the same illness, Schiele died three days later. He was only 28.

Egon Schiele, self-portrait from 1912.

As the pandemic tore through Europe and the world, public gathering places were shuttered – theatres, cinemas, restaurants, cafés. The First World War had already put paid to the golden days of the Habsburg-era coffee house scene, and as the flu brought its terrifying death toll, those days must have seemed even more distant to the inhabitants of Vienna.

In the 1920s, unable to afford rising rents, some well-known coffee houses closed, their premises taken over by the growing number of bank branches … but Café Sperl, haven of daring artists and birthplace of the Vienna Secession, was a survivor.

The nebbish and his henchmen take over

The following decade saw the rise to power in Germany of Adolf Hitler, and the intensification of the Nazis' brutality towards the country's Jews. Nevertheless, the Jews of Vienna, some at least, still felt safe from what was happening next door. In the early days of the Third Reich they shared a joke in which a Jewish businessman tells his wife how he imagines the Führer will end up:

> He'll be going around our coffee house, shabbily dressed, looking for newspapers to read. And you'll say, 'Isn't he that fellow Hitler, that nebbish?' And he'll come to our table and ask, 'Excuse me, is *Die Presse* free?' And I'll say, 'Not for you, Herr Hitler, not for you!'

The joking stopped in March 1938 with the Anschluss, Austria's occupation and its annexation into Hitler's Reich. Jews who did not flee in time were now subject to ever-increasing persecution, and the free, intellectual and creative spirit of Viennese coffee house culture was extinguished. The Nazis considered the Viennese coffee house a 'Jewish institution' and despised the humour, wit and irony that were staple ingredients of the cerebral atmosphere they generated. As soon as they took control of the city, the cafés were either 'Aryanised' and made amenable to Nazi Party members, or closed down. Even profitable cafés were liquidated on the false pretext of bankruptcy.

As for the groundbreaking artists of the Vienna Secession, they fared just as badly. On becoming Chancellor in 1933, Hitler ordered the authorities to seize any artwork he didn't like, in other words, anything not conforming to the traditional, classical ideals of human beauty. Symbolist art, Expressionist art – basically, all Modernist art – was deemed 'degenerate' and expropriated, sold at auction, or destroyed. Of course, the work of Schiele and Klimt fell into that category.

How Hitler must have hated (and envied) Schiele in particular – the talented teenager who breezed into the elite art academy from which *he* had been excluded, then proceeded to make a name for himself with his outrageous, subversive work and win the approbation and friendship of no less than the celebrated Gustav Klimt. The Nazis destroyed the beautiful Secession Building itself, as a representation of degenerate art. But after the Second World War it was faithfully reconstructed and is today the headquarters and exhibition hall of the Vienna Secession, which is still very much in existence.

Klimt's glittering portrait of Adele Bloch-Bauer, known as *The Woman in Gold*, was seized by the Nazis; after the war it was put on show in a prestigious Vienna gallery, which refused to admit the painting had been stolen from its rightful owner. In 2006, after a seven-year legal battle and a ruling by the United States Supreme Court, the Bloch-Bauer family finally won back ownership of the painting. Sold at auction the same year, it fetched $135 million – then a world record for a painting – and is now on display in a New York gallery. Not bad going for a 'degenerate'.

Apart from a few slightly incongruous modern pictures on the walls, the Café Sperl has admirably maintained its traditional late nineteenth-century Viennese coffee house style, and won a string of café-related awards over the years. It's a good choice for those who prefer the cosy to the grand, and somewhere off the bustling tourist beat.

Chapter Nine

NEW YORK CAFÉ, BUDAPEST

The Ottoman Turks' occupation of the Kingdom of Hungary from 1541 to 1699 wasn't a rosy period for the Hungarian people, the Magyars. The population was decimated through deportations, slave raids, massacres and famines. The economy was wrecked. All lands were appropriated for the use of the Ottoman rulers, their soldiers and administrators, with the natives bled white by taxes. The royal palace in Buda was allowed to fall into ruin.

On the other hand, they did introduce two fine Turkish customs that have been deeply ingrained in Hungarian culture ever since: the Turkish bath, utilising the region's natural hot thermal springs, and coffee drinking. Indeed, the Hungarian word for coffee, *kávé*, stems directly from the Turkish *kahve*.

The Turks had finally been routed by the armies of the Habsburg-led Holy Roman Empire, but that didn't mean independence for Hungary; the country now fell under Habsburg domination. It seemed it was the fate of this central European nation to be overrun and controlled by bigger and more ruthless powers – the Mongols, the Turks, the Austrians, and later on, the Nazis and the Soviets. That's what comes, in part at least, from an unfortunate geography: lying on a vulnerable plain in the path of ambitious, rampaging peoples from both east and west.

In the eighteenth century, the Habsburg rulers colonised Hungary with large numbers of peasants from all over Europe, especially Slovaks, Serbs, Croatians and Germans. The country's population more than tripled, to 8 million, but only 39 per cent of its people were Magyars. The country had long had a legislative body, a parliament called a Diet, which convened in the city of Pressburg (now Bratislava in Slovakia). But its powers were limited. The Habsburgs were in overall control, ruling Hungary as a conquered territory.

The Holy Roman Emperor, Leopold I, redistributed lands freed from the Turks, and Hungarians considered disloyal to the Habsburg crown lost their estates. The land seizures, as well as the Catholic Habsburgs' repression of Hungary's Protestant population, frustrated the Hungarians. So it was predictable enough that an uprising was on the cards. In 1703, a Hungarian nobleman with the title Prince of Transylvania, Ferenc Rákóczi, spearheaded a war of independence against Habsburg rule that was to last eight years. Fighting alongside the nobles were high-ranking liberals, former soldiers and the peasantry. Alas, it turned out to be only one of Hungary's failed revolutions …

A century later, following Austria's defeat in 1805 by Napoleon Bonaparte at the Battle of Austerlitz, the Holy Roman Empire was dissolved. The last of its emperors, Francis II, had already formed the Austrian Empire, encompassing all the territories ruled by the Habsburg monarchy, and proclaimed himself Francis I, Emperor of Austria. All the chopping and changing of empires and emperors didn't help Hungary much because, in essence, its overlord was the same: Austria's House of Habsburg. And the grievances against this unwanted foreign control continued.

By the middle of the nineteenth century, a revolutionary spirit was in the air all around the Austrian Empire. Much of it was to do with growing nationalist fervour within its assorted ethnic constituents – Poles, Czechs, Slovaks, Slovenes, Serbs, Croats, Ukrainians, etc. They were after some form of autonomy, if not outright independence from Austria, and perhaps even supremacy over a neighbour – this is a region of endless ethnic rivalries. But there was another factor too. Political and social tensions had been increasing, with the more liberal-minded leaders and citizens opposing the deep-rooted conservatism that had been moving this absolutist empire further away from the ideals of the Enlightenment. The year 1848 saw the outbreak of the anti-Habsburg revolutions, a phenomenon that came to be known as the Springtime of Nations. Arguably, the most dramatic revolution of them all was that in Hungary – it was also the only one to begin, quite literally, in a coffee house.

It's now or never

The Pilvax Coffee House was a spacious venue with pillars and a vaulted ceiling, situated in the heart of the inner city in Pest. It was named after its Austrian owner, Karl Pillwax, who had learnt the art of coffee making in Vienna, moved to Budapest, married a Hungarian girl and taken over the coffee house in 1842. He had the portraits of historic Hungarian heroes painted on the walls, which was perhaps why – in this era of growing patriotism – the café drew young artists, poets, intellectuals and students of a rebellious, anti-Habsburg inclination. (Its billiard tables were an added attraction.)

Two sets of friends made it their regular retreat. One consisted of the young poet Sándor Petőfi and his circle, who called themselves the Tízek Társasága (Society of Ten). The other comprised law students and intellectuals centred on the (even younger) writer Pál Vasvári. In 1846, they joined forces as Fiatal Magyarország, the Young Hungary movement.

Petőfi was the lynchpin of the revolution in Budapest. During intense meetings at the Pilvax in March 1848, he co-wrote the vital Twelve Points document, setting out the key demands of the Hungarian people. These included an independent Hungarian Parliament, freedom of the press and an end to censorship, as well as universal equal rights under the law, the release of political prisoners and the abolition

The Pilvax Coffee House in Budapest, in its nineteenth-century heyday.

of serfdom. In a direct echo of the French Revolution, it ended with the rallying cry: 'Equality, freedom, brotherhood!' Petőfi also composed the revolutionary poem, 'Nemzeti Dal' (National Song), which inspired his compatriots to rise up:

> On your feet, Hungarian, the Homeland is calling!
> The time has come, it's now or never!
> Shall we be slaves or free men?
> That's the question, now answer!
> On the god of the Hungarians, we swear,
> We swear we shall be slaves no more!

Early on the morning of 15 March, Petőfi and his fellow rebels met at the Pilvax. After downing their customary black coffee, they began marching around the streets of Pest, reciting Petőfi's poem and reading out the Twelve Points to a growing throng. Then they hastened to a printer's, where they had thousands of copies made of both the document and the poem, for distribution to the public. Later that morning, crowds entered the Town Hall and forced the mayor to sign the Twelve Points. Then, to great cheers, Petőfi addressed a mass gathering from the steps of the National Museum. Later, he and his adherents crossed the Danube to Buda, where they confronted the imperial governing council, the representatives of Emperor Ferdinand, and made them sign it too.

At the time, Austria had its own problems with the revolution that had broken out only two days earlier in Vienna, so Emperor Ferdinand, yielding to pressure, conceded the revolutionaries' demands. The Twelve Points, renamed the March Laws, received royal assent and to all intents and purposes, Hungary became an independent state. A new government was set up, quickly approving a sweeping package of reforms, which created a political system based on parliamentary democracy.

The trouble arose later in the year, when the emperor abdicated and was succeeded by his nephew, Franz Joseph, who arbitrarily (and illegally) revoked the Hungarian reform laws ratified by his predecessor. Austria ordered imperial forces to invade

Sándor Petőfi, Magyar poet and revolutionary of 1848.

Hungary and a full-throttled war of independence began, in which the newly formed Hungarian Revolutionary Army, the Honvéd, won some notable victories. (The Pilvax itself contained an army recruiting office.) Now the country's multi-ethnic composition proved a boon: the Magyars were supported by most of the Slovaks, Germans, Slovenes and Jews living on Hungarian territory. They were duly rewarded. In July 1849, Hungary's Revolutionary Parliament proclaimed and enacted Europe's first laws guaranteeing ethnic and minority rights.

That summer, after a series of major defeats, the Austrian Empire was on the brink of collapse. A desperate Emperor Franz Joseph called for help from the Russians and Tsar Nicholas responded by sending an army 280,000 strong. The joint forces of Russia and Austria at last defeated the Hungarians, who were forced to capitulate on 13 August 1849. After Habsburg power was restored, Hungary was placed under martial law.

Sándor Petőfi, who had joined the Hungarian Revolutionary Army, had already been killed in the previous month's Battle of Segesvár. He was 26 years old. His friend from the Pilvax and revolutionary comrade, Pál Vasvári, had also fallen in battle; he was 22.

Despite the revolution's failure, it remains for the people of Hungary one of the most significant events in their troubled, thousand-year history. The date of its outbreak, 15 March, is a national holiday. And its close association with the Pilvax coffee house has not been forgotten. During the revolution, Petőfi renamed it Szabadság Csarnok (Freedom Hall). But after the Hungarian defeat the coffee house fell under new management and lost its lustre as the cradle of patriotic rebellion … until the 1867 Compromise ushered in a golden era for a new empire, Austria Hungary. The Pilvax was then resurrected as a kind of national shrine. Its new owner covered the walls once more with Magyar heroes – this time from 1848 – and a memorial plaque above the door reminded everyone that it was the spot where Petőfi first recited his legendary poem and the revolutionaries of the Young Hungary movement compiled their list of demands.

But prestige, sadly, could not save the Pilvax. One outcome of the dual monarchy was a vast programme of construction in downtown Pest, involving the demolition of many earlier buildings. In 1910, urban planners decided to knock down the whole block of which the Pilvax was a part. With a mournful farewell ceremony attended by a large number of its faithful customers, the Pilvax closed its doors for good in 1911. For two years, it stood forlornly with boarded-up windows and doors, before being knocked down.

Throwing away the key

Today there is a modern Pilvax café and restaurant, even a Pilvax hotel, on the same street (the aptly named Pilvax Passage) and more or less same site as the original coffee house. They make the most of their historic namesake by commemorating

Hungary's noble 1848 Revolution with artwork on the walls and a plaque. But only the name is the same; this twenty-first-century incarnation unfortunately can't conjure up visions of the past. Which is why this chapter is not headed Pilvax Café, but New York Café – because the latter most definitely can.

This opulent, glamorous nineteenth-century establishment in the centre of Budapest has a personal significance for me – and not just because my family came from Hungary and Budapest is the city of my birth. I first went to the café in 1980, while visiting the country to do research for my first book. This was during the communist era, of course, and Mikhail Gorbachev's reforms were still a few years away. The place was then called the Hungária, as 'New York', a name strongly suggestive of Western capitalism, was hardly on the communists' approved list. And it was state-owned, like everything else.

I was taken there by my dear, now long-departed relatives, Mári and Dódi – my mother's cousins. As we sat there sipping espressos they explained that my Budapest-born father, when a young writer and man-about-town, used to meet his friends and colleagues at the New York. I later recounted the episode in my book, *The Paper Bridge*:

> 'For a while your father actually used to work in this building,' Dódi told me. 'He wrote for a weekly paper which had its offices upstairs above the café. Of course the place was badly damaged during the Second World War, and it remained closed for years …'
>
> I looked around. There was a marble floor, elaborately gilded walls and ceiling, neo-classical paintings and carved figures, huge mirrors and globe lights. But I was disappointed. There were no animated groups of writers huddled over black coffee and pálinka, blowing smoke high up to the painted cherubs …
>
> 'Do you know,' Dódi was saying, 'at one time the waiters here brought pencils and paper along with the coffee. This was where all the writers, the newspapermen, theatre directors and producers used to meet. Famous people.'
>
> But the place was empty now except for a tableful of Arabs and two spotty youths flirting with a waitress. I was obviously born after my time.

Throughout the nineteenth century, Budapest had been developing into an impressive, cosmopolitan European capital, strongly influenced not only by Vienna, but also by Paris and London. Its iconic bridge across the Danube, the elegant Chain Bridge – the first to link Buda with Pest – was designed by the English engineer William Tierney Clark. A grander version of Tierney Clark's Marlow Bridge across the Thames, it was shipped from the UK to Budapest for its final construction, completed in 1849. The city's premier boulevard, Andrássy Avenue, dates from 1876. Lined with stunning Neo-Renaissance mansions and townhouses,

Budapest's Café New York on the ground floor of the grand New York Life Insurance Company, at the end of the nineteenth century.

The opulent interior of the New York Café, Budapest, 1896.

it was modelled on Paris's Champs-Élysées and is now a UNESCO World Heritage Site. Inspired by the London Underground – the world's first underground electrified railway system, which opened in 1890 – Budapest inaugurated its own underground Metro only six years later, the world's second. The resplendent Neo-Gothic Parliament, built on the riverfront in Pest, took as its model the Palace of Westminster; it was completed in 1902.

By the end of the nineteenth century, there were some 600 coffee houses in Budapest. But the Neo-Renaissance New York Café, opened in 1894 on a section of the inner city ring road called the Elizabeth Boulevard, was the most palatial. And no wonder – it was designed by the same renowned architect, Alajos Hauszmann, who was in charge of the reconstruction of Buda Castle. Its name came from the fact that it occupied the ground floor of the building that housed the local branch of the New York Life Insurance Company.

The interior of the New York Café was cavernous, with a lower level in the middle nicknamed 'the deep water', for dining and live music. As soon as it opened its doors, it was a magnet for the literati of the day. There's an old story (apocryphal perhaps) about a bunch of enthusiastic young writers who, having spent many happy hours in this splendid new watering hole, decided they loved it so much they didn't want it to close. So they ran off with the front door key and threw it in the Danube, forcing the place to stay open all night.

What is in no doubt is that the golden epoch of Austria-Hungary was a magnificent time for literature. Of course, those writing in German were much more fortunate: it's a world language. Hungarian, on the other hand, is a victim of its isolation amongst the major language groups, being unrelated to the Latin, Germanic or Slavic tongues. This has kept it more or less imprisoned within its own small country and its diaspora of native speakers. Yet scores of top-class Magyar novelists, poets and playwrights were creating their works during that era. Only a handful overcame the linguistic barrier. One such was the playwright Ferenc Molnár, a New York Café regular in the early twentieth century, who later emigrated to America. His play *The Guardsman* was turned into a 1931 Hollywood film starring Alfred Lunt and Lynn Fontanne, and the 1945 Rodgers and Hammerstein musical *Carousel* was based on his play *Liliom*.

Writers from all over Hungary gravitated to Budapest, not merely because of the proximity of the editors and publishers they hoped would buy their work, but because the very atmosphere of the city, its colours and sounds and vibrancy, fed their creativity. And the New York Café was celebrated for its generous attitude to its literary customers. There was an inexpensive dish devised specifically for struggling scribes. Consisting of cold meats, cheeses and bread, even its modest price was often waived by soft-hearted waiters, who also lent money to writers in need of cash. Naturally, paper was provided gratis, along with ink (the supply of free ink was stopped only after the café's irrepressible habitué, Frigyes Karinthy, spilled half a bottle of it on a grey sofa; the ink was replaced with pencils).

As in Vienna, writers often spent all day at the café, a welcome refuge from their shabby little rented rooms. They could send and receive messages and letters from there, avail themselves of the scores of Hungarian and foreign newspapers hanging from bamboo racks, and get their work done – articles, short stories, even entire novels were written amidst the chatter, clatter and swirling smoke of the New York Café.

The multi-faceted writer Dezső Kosztolányi often wove the café into his writings: 'You, New York coffee house, where I spent so many days,' one of his poems begins. He recalls how, in his youth, the café gave him and others free coffee in return for poems, 'allowing young writers to come, dream and smoke endless cigarettes'. Another writer, Jenő Rákosi, remarked: 'every intelligent person spent a part of his youth in the coffee house … without that, the education of a young man would be imperfect and incomplete.' Author Jenő Heltai recounted: 'In the lavish New York Café, you got your shoes polished, your clothes ironed, could get a shave, a haircut and a manicure at all hours … and if it came to it, lodgings and overnight accommodation too.'

Men of the literary world gather at the New York Café in Budapest, *c.*1890s.

It was most pithily summed up by Sándor Márai: 'No café, no literature.' (His novel *Embers*, conveying nostalgia for the bygone multicultural society of the Austro-Hungarian Empire, was adapted for the stage by Christopher Hampton and performed in London in 2006.)

These were also glory days for newspapers, made possible by freedom of the press during the epoch of the dual monarchy. There were twenty-odd Hungarian-language national papers in Budapest in the year 1900, as well as numerous literary periodicals. One of them, *Nyugat* (*West*), was of particular significance. Founded in 1908, it published both poetry and prose, and was inspired by the philosophies, movements and styles then current in Western Europe: Naturalism, Symbolism, Impressionism, Expressionism. The first Hungarian-language journal to discuss philosophers such as Nietzsche and Kierkegaard, it had a significant impact on Hungarian scientists and intellectuals who later had flourishing careers outside Hungary.

Alongside the important male writers of the day whose work it carried, *Nyugat* published the writing of Hungary's first major female author, Margit Kaffka. A full-time contributor to the journal, her best known book, *Színek és évek* (*Colours and Years*), appeared in 1912. She wrote about the physical and spiritual hardships endured by women attempting to live independent lives in the early twentieth century, with its increasingly anachronistic societal attitudes. But soon after establishing her reputation and winning the admiration of her male peers, she died – together with her young son – in the 1918 Spanish Flu epidemic.

Nyugat was an emblematic title. The truth is that Hungarians have always looked westwards for inspiration – this is why so many of them reject their country's geographical positioning within 'Eastern' Europe, placing it firmly within the sphere of Central Europe instead. It was only the twentieth-century aberration (and abomination) of Soviet control that caused the Stalinist-minded segment of the population to take their cue from the East.

Showbiz glamour

Besides the literati, the New York Café attracted a great many people involved in the theatre, as well as the nascent film industry, and contracts were often negotiated and signed at its tables. In the 1920s, the fame of certain Hungarian actors and actresses had reached Hollywood, and a string of movie moguls travelled to Budapest in search of talent. Louis B. Mayer, Samuel Goldwyn and Adolph Zukor (himself Hungarian-born) were among those to visit the New York Café for meetings with them.

One such meeting took place in 1925 between Sam Goldwyn and 24-year-old actress Vilma Bánky, who had already made a handful of Hungarian and German films. So impressed was the big shot producer that he signed her there and then and swept her off to Hollywood. She went on to achieve considerable success there during the silent film era, her beauty winning her the epithet of 'the Hungarian Rhapsody'. The silent film star and leading heartthrob Rudolph Valentino was enthralled by her and chose her as his leading lady; she appeared opposite him in *The Eagle* in 1925, and the *The Son of the Sheik* a year later. Then sadly, the screen partnership was brought to an abrupt end, with Valentino's death of peritonitis at the age of 31.

Then there were the Hungarian film directors. John Lukacs, perhaps the finest English-language chronicler of golden-era Budapest, writes in his book *Budapest 1900*: 'the careers of such world-famous movie producers and directors as Alexander Korda and Michael Curtiz began in that noisy, rapid-fire of the Elizabeth Ring, in the smoky hurly-burly and sometimes tawdry glitter of the New York Café.'

Silent film star Vilma Bánky, signed by movie mogul Sam Goldwyn at the New York Café in Budapest, and swept off to Hollywood.

Curtiz went on to direct, most famously, the Hollywood wartime classic *Casablanca*, starring Humphrey Bogart and Ingrid Bergman and featuring a large cast of genuine refugee actors from Europe. On the American Film Institute's list of the 'One Hundred Greatest American Movies of All Time', it is ranked second, after *Citizen Kane*.

Korda, meanwhile, settled in England and in 1942 was knighted by George VI – the first film director to receive the honour – for his contribution to the war effort. During a sojourn in Hollywood two years earlier, he had shot *That Hamilton Woman*, starring Laurence Olivier and Vivien Leigh. Its subject was Britain's struggle against Napoleon, i.e. resistance to a dictator who seeks to dominate the world, but its parallels with the then war against the Nazis were not lost on audiences, and it was powerful propaganda. Britain was desperate to win the support of America in the period before Pearl Harbor forced its entry into the war.

Korda also aided Britain in another, more covert way. While making the film, his offices supplied cover to MI5 agents gathering intelligence on German activities in America and on isolationist politicians and pressure groups such as the America First Committee. He carried out this secret role in collaboration with Winston Churchill, whom Korda knew well: before the war, he had signed Churchill as a screenwriter and historical advisor on his films, and they had liked working together. Churchill later claimed that Korda was 'the only honourable man in the world of film', and that *That Hamilton Woman* was his all-time favourite movie.

After my first visit to the New York Café, during communist times, it would be many years before I returned. When I did, the experience couldn't have been more different. The world had changed, and the café along with it. With the fall of communism, it regained its old name, the state sold it to an Italian hotel chain, and the building was fully renovated. A luxury hotel was created above the meticulously restored ground-floor café. The building is now known as the New York Palace and the café's gilded splendour would impress Emperor Franz Joseph himself, should he magically reappear.

In the eyes of the world, Budapest has been transformed from a little-known ex-communist satellite state, with an obscure culture and arcane language, into one of the most appealing of city-break and holiday destinations. Accordingly, its streets teem with visitors from virtually every nation, and a standard item on the tourist agenda is the New York Café, perhaps because it is so often described as the most beautiful café in the world. These days, it's generally full of tourists and visiting business people. But not exclusively so …

When I went there in 2015, it was to have coffee with an old friend of my father's, the writer and historian Tamás Ungvári. The New York was abuzz that day with customers tucking into fancy cakes and desserts. Tourists, yes, but Tamás assured me it was still a place where he and his literary pals liked to gather occasionally. For old times' sake, perhaps. It was definitely a lot pricier than in the old days, and a hard-up scribe would be ill-advised to ask for a loan from one of the waiters. And yet, as I looked around I could sense a trace of the former mystique lingering on, amid the (now smoke-free) golden opulence. The ghosts of past novelists and poets, actresses and movie moguls had not, perhaps, been vanquished completely.

The café remains determined to keep this past alive. Among its hundred or so glass-topped square tables are nine that are larger than the rest and decorated with photos and stories, poems and quotes, relating to illustrious past regulars. One of these tables is dedicated to playwright Ferenc Molnár. And another to my father's friend, Tamás Ungvári, who died a few years ago.

Chapter Ten

CAFÉ DE FLORE, PARIS

The Café de Flore, on the Boulevard Saint-Germain, opened its doors in 1887. It was named after the sculpture of Flora, the Roman goddess of flowers and springtime, which once stood on the opposite side of the boulevard. In lieu of the statue, the café these days displays a profusion of foliage above its white and green awnings.

The Left Bank district in which it lies, Saint-Germain-des-Prés, has long been known as a bohemian and intellectual quarter in Paris, home to musicians, artists and writers, all drawn to its legendary cafés and bistros. Besides the Flore there is its long-time rival and near next-door neighbour, the Café les Deux Magots (named after the two antique statues of inscrutable Chinamen that adorn the café's interior); the Brasserie Lipp, directly across the street, where Ernest Hemingway often lunched in the 1920s; and the august Café Procope. Oscar Wilde, recently released from Reading Gaol and impoverished, spent his last days in this neighbourhood at the shabby little Hotel d'Alsace on the Rue des Beaux-Arts. It is still there, now called simply L'Hotel, but these days is a luxurious 'boutique' establishment well out of reach of down-at-heel poets and playwrights.

The Deux Magots has a glittering history as a twentieth-century rendezvous spot for celebrated literary and artistic figures, for thinkers and creators. But the Flore can perhaps lay claim to an even greater reputation, as the place where more 'isms' came into being (Surrealism, Existentialism), more books were written (such as Simone de Beauvoir's feminist tract *The Second Sex*) and more publications founded.

But back to the beginning. By the end of the nineteenth century, the Flore had become a popular hub for writers and philosophers. One of the regulars was the political theorist Charles Maurras, a complicated and contentious figure who joined a political movement called Action Française and became its leading ideologue. It was a nationalist, monarchist movement, anti-parliamentary – an all-out reaction against the legacy of the French Revolution – advocating, rather unrealistically, a restoration of the royal dynasty of the House of Bourbon. From 1908, the movement's daily newspaper was edited by Maurras. Years later, upstairs at the Café de Flore, he composed his tome *Au Signe de Flore* (*At the Sign of Flore*) about the early years of the Action Française.

Café de Flore, Paris, *c.*1900.

Maurras was a jumble of contradictions. He was a strong supporter of the Catholic Church, but one who had himself lost his Catholic faith and turned agnostic. Having spent several months in jail for making death threats against the Jewish socialist politician Leon Blum, he was nonetheless mocked by fascists for rejecting violence as a means of furthering the cause of Action Française. And he was an anti-Semite who supported Marshal Pétain's collaborationist regime during the Second World War, whilst opposing the Nazis' racist policies and the deportation of Jews. After the fall of the Vichy government in 1944, Maurras was sentenced to life imprisonment. Reprieved on health grounds in 1952, he died later that year.

Today, Maurras is regarded as an influential right-wing political theorist of twentieth-century Europe, perhaps the most important French conservative intellectual of his generation. He remains controversial, attacked by those on the left as a 'fascist icon' for his anti-Semitism and support of Vichy, whilst the conservative George Pompidou, who served as both Prime Minister and President of France in the 1960s and 1970s, regarded Maurras as 'a prophet of the modern world'. French President Emmanuel Macron, in a 2020 interview with the French magazine *L'Express* in which he discussed issues regarding French identity and culture, said: 'I fight all the anti-Semitic ideas of Maurras, but I find it absurd to say that Maurras must no longer exist.'

As for Action Française, it was dissolved in 1944 but only three years later made a comeback, and has been through various iterations since, with new publications and new political affiliations. It's tiny now, with a membership of about 3,000, and sees itself as a think tank rather than a political party, presenting its own answers to issues regarding national sovereignty, the economy, globalisation, etc. It promotes classical French culture and traditional Catholic values. As a nationalist movement, it is naturally anti-EU, putting the interests of the nation above all other concerns, in accordance with its motto: 'All that is national is ours'. It remains fervently royalist too. Nearly two and a half centuries after the French Revolution, the conflict between republicanism and monarchism has, it seems, still not been entirely laid to rest in France.

It was Surreal

In 1912, the poet Guillaume Apollinaire founded his literary and artistic review, *Les Soirées de Paris*, at the Café de Flore together with André Salmon, a critic and fellow poet. They turned the café's first floor into their editorial offices. Pablo Picasso, Henri Matisse and Georges Braque were among the avant-garde artists who contributed illustrations. Apollinaire was of Polish descent (original name Wilhelm Albert Włodzimierz Apolinary Kostrowicki) but born in Rome; his new name he had adopted after immigrating to France in his late teens.

Unfortunately, his arts review didn't last long, as the outbreak of the First World War two years later put an end to it. He joined the French Army and was posted to the front in the spring of 1915. A year later, receiving a serious shrapnel wound to his temple, he was invalided out of the army, and it was straight back to the Café de Flore. He would arrive early in the morning so as to install himself next to the café's heater, and spend the day there, writing and meeting friends. Most significantly, these included the poets André Breton, Louis Aragon and Paul Éluard. Strongly influenced by Apollinaire, they would create the movement that came to be known as Surrealism. Breton, the movement's principal theorist, and Aragon claimed they invented it at a table at the Flore in 1917. Its aim was to release the unbridled power of the imagination and the subconscious, and of dreams – pure psychic automatism, as Breton put it.

The term Surrealism itself was first used by Apollinaire in March of that year, in connection with a new ballet called *Parade*. Choreographed by Léonide Massine, with music by Erik Satie and a one-act scenario by Jean Cocteau, Apollinaire described this composition created for Sergei Diaghilev's Ballets Russes as 'a kind of surrealism' in the programme notes he wrote for the ballet. Thus with a stroke of his pen he coined the word shortly to be applied to this emerging artistic movement, which a decade later included among its adherents Salvador Dalí and his fellow Spaniard, the film director Luis Buñuel.

Today, the progenitor of Surrealism, Apollinaire, is considered one of the leading poets of the early twentieth century. Art, he believed, should not be based on any theory or 'school', but the act of creating should rather stem from personal intuition and imagination. Apollinaire did things no one had ever done before but others have copied since, such as writing poetry without punctuation – to his thinking, any rule of grammar could be ignored. And he produced one of the earliest Surrealist literary works, the play *The Breasts of Tiresias*, which has remarkably apposite echoes for our own times, with its themes of transgenderism and feminism. Inspired by the ancient Greek myth about the blind Theban soothsayer Teiresias, it tells the story of Thérèse, who changes her sex to obtain power among men in order to subvert conventions and establish equality between the sexes.

Apollinaire never fully recovered from his war wound. In 1918, still in weakened health, he fell victim to the Spanish Flu pandemic, dying in November of that year at the age of 38. But the style of Surrealism, in art, in photography, in filmmaking and literature, has endured well into the twenty-first century – everyone understands instinctively what it means.

Lost, boozy and with no respect

The post-First World War period saw the arrival in Paris of the 'Lost Generation'. They were writers (mainly American) experiencing the aftershock of war, a sense of aimlessness, disillusionment and grief. Friends and family members had died in the war, an innocence had been lost, and priorities recalibrated. American society was felt to be puritanical, restricting and insular – an unsuitable environment for creativity. As the epicentre of cultural and social freedom, it was to Paris that these expats flocked in the 1920s. They included aspiring novelist Ernest Hemingway, who had been seriously wounded while driving a Red Cross ambulance in Italy during the war; the already successful F. Scott Fitzgerald, exemplar of the Jazz Age, working on the novel that would become his masterpiece, *The Great Gatsby*; the painter and free-form poet e.e. cummings (he eschewed capital letters); and the modernist poet Ezra Pound, whose eccentricities were described thus by English writer Ford Maddox Ford: 'He would wear trousers made of green billiard cloth, a pink coat, a blue shirt, a tie hand-painted by a Japanese friend, an immense sombrero, a flaming beard cut to a point, and a single, large blue earring.' (Pound later went insane and was committed to an asylum.)

The experimental writer and art collector Gertrude Stein was their forerunner. She moved to Paris from America in 1903, spending the rest of her life there and setting up home with her lesbian lover, Alice B. Toklas. It was at her celebrated Saturday evening salon that many of the expat writers and artists, established or up-and-coming, met each other and shared their ideas. And she was the one who coined the expression 'lost generation' to describe Hemingway and his contemporaries, when she told him one day: 'All of you young people who served in the war, you are a lost generation … you have no respect for anything. You drink yourselves to death.'

The Lost Generation in 1920s Paris – a smiling Ernest Hemingway sitting between his first wife, Hadley, on right, and second wife, Pauline.

Hemingway disagreed with her assessment but was struck by the phrase 'lost generation' and used it as an epigraph to his first novel, *The Sun Also Rises*, about a cluster of war-battered, angst-ridden and disaffected expats in Paris, who had complex romantic and sexual entanglements, much as Hemingway and his friends did. 'Everyone was drinking all the time and everyone was having affairs all the time,' Hemingway's wife, Hadley Richardson, later recalled. 'I found it sort of upsetting.' As well she might: Hemingway eventually left her for Pauline Pfeiffer, with whom he'd been having an affair. And Stein wasn't far off the mark: Fitzgerald did ultimately drink himself to death.

However it has been described, that generation produced some of the most highly regarded and enduring writing of the twentieth century. Hemingway went on to win the Nobel Prize in Literature. *The Great Gatsby*, meanwhile, is a classic that has sold 30 million copies since first published by Fitzgerald in 1925 and has been turned into a movie no fewer than five times.

Besides Stein's weekly salon, the expat novelists and poets regularly retreated to their favoured cafés, to meet each other or to work. The Flore and the Deux Magots, neighbours in Saint-Germain-des-Prés, were much frequented by the lost generation. The two cafés had retained their reputation as the haunts of innovative figures on the literary and artistic scene, and as places of debate amongst intellectuals and politicos. But Hemingway's 'home café' was La Closerie des Lilas (the lilac enclosure), a little further south in the district of Montparnasse: 'It was warm inside in the winter and in the spring and fall it was very fine outside with the tables under the shade of the trees,' he wrote in his memoir of Paris, *A Moveable Feast*. He spent hours there each morning writing short stories, hoping Ezra Pound wouldn't turn up for breakfast and interrupt him. His rudeness about some of the other famous cafés in Montparnasse is on record: the Rotonde was where 'the scum of Greenwich Village, New York, has been skimmed off and deposited in large ladles', and the Sélect was nothing but 'a collection of inmates'. Le Dôme was all right, because it was frequented by 'people who worked' rather than tourists. He said that he liked those who 'went to the big cafés because they were lost in them and no one noticed them and they could be alone in them and be together'. (Not dissimilar to the sentiment expressed by writer Iris Murdoch decades later: 'I hate solitude but I am afraid of intimacy. The company I need is the company which a pub or a café will provide.')

The American expats' spell in their cherished City of Light didn't last very long. The stock market crash of October 1929 brought with it a global economic collapse and the Great Depression. It became much harder to make money, the cost of living went up, and the carefree, independent life of the artist was no longer sustainable. There was an air of anxiety, and the writers and artists started to go home. Within a few years, the community had dispersed. Only Gertrude Stein stayed behind, dying in 1946 at the American Hospital in a suburb of Paris.

But Hemingway's years in Paris, both happy and troubled, stayed with him the rest of his life and gave his posthumously published memoir its title: 'If you are lucky enough to have lived in Paris as a young man, then wherever you go for the rest of your life, it stays with you, for Paris is a moveable feast.'

On being existential

During the Second World War, a new cadre of writers and thinkers settled into the Café de Flore: the Existentialists. It appears that the establishment's main draw and its advantage over its rival the Deux Magots and other Left Bank cafés was to do with temperature. In 1939, the Flore's new manager, Paul Boubal, installed a bigger and more powerful coal-fired heater, an upgrade highly popular with locals living in their chilly apartments.

At the outbreak of the war, Jean-Paul Sartre and Simone de Beauvoir, two budding writer-philosophers (and lovers with a famously open relationship) were scribbling away at their novels at one or other of their usual café hangouts in Montparnasse, Le Dôme or La Rotonde. One day, after Sartre had been called up for military service, de Beauvoir was on her way home when she decided to stop off at the Flore for a coffee. Struck by how delightfully warm it was inside, she resolved to make it her new place to write, and arrived early each morning to claim a table next to the heater. When Sartre returned in 1941 (after his capture by the Germans and nine months as a POW), he joined de Beauvoir there and they resumed their daily writing routine together.

By then, Paris had been occupied by the Nazis for a year and as they increasingly appropriated the city's stocks of food and fuel, the Parisians themselves suffered from all kinds of shortages. The Dôme was now overrun by German soldiers, Sartre observed bitterly, who brought along their own tea and coffee for the café to prepare specially for them, whilst locals had to make do with awful ersatz versions. Perhaps because they were less famous at the time, the cafés in Saint-Germain-des-Prés attracted fewer Wehrmacht soldiers than those in Montparnasse, so the Flore remained relatively Nazi-free. This made for a more relaxed atmosphere for its habitués, who reportedly said the place 'smelled like freedom'.

Sartre and de Beauvoir turned the Flore into their headquarters/office during the day and their social centre/meeting room at night. Sartre wrote:

> We got completely settled here: from 9 a.m. till noon we worked here, then we went for a lunch, and at 2 p.m. we came back and talked with friends till eight in the evening. After the dinner we arranged meetings with friends here. It can seem strange, but we are at home at Café de Flore.

Because it was less busy upstairs, they took to working at separate tables in the room on the first floor. Paul Boubal didn't mind these two 'pillars of the Flore' being there all day without consuming much food or drink. Allegedly, he even allowed Sartre to install a special telephone line for his calls. De Beauvoir later recalled: 'Even when the air raid sirens sounded, we merely pretended to make our way down to the basement, but in fact crept back up to the first floor where we carried on with our work.' (Perhaps her insouciance regarding air raids was due to the fact that Paris was bombed very little during the war.)

In time, they were joined by other intellectuals, until the first floor was peopled almost entirely by thinkers and theorists brooding over the deeper questions of life and working on their philosophical writings. In 1943, Sartre and de Beauvoir met Albert Camus, who became part of their intellectual circle.

De Beauvoir's first novel, *She Came to Stay*, a fictionalised account of the wartime ménage à trois between her, Sartre and a French actress, was published during the war and brought her much attention. It was a dabble in existential themes revolving around personal freedom and the relationship between the self and 'the other'. People began turning up ad hoc at the Flore in order to speak to her. Growing tired of the interruptions, she insisted that everyone book a fifteen-minute appointment for a more convenient time of day.

It was during these years that Sartre and de Beauvoir forged the principles of Existentialism, an exploration of the meaning of human existence. What is

Existentialists at the Café de Flore, with Jean-Paul Sartre, on the left, and Simone de Beauvoir, on the right.

its purpose, its value? How does one define virtue? How does one deal with a world that can seem pointless and absurd? The roots of this type of philosophical examination go back further, of course, to nineteenth-century European thinkers who shared the same concerns: most notably, the Danish theologian Søren Kierkegaard, generally considered the first Existentialist philosopher, though the term hadn't yet been invented. He proposed that each individual – not society, religious orthodoxy, our political rulers or any other authority – is responsible for giving meaning to his or her life, and for living it accordingly. Others who strongly influenced the Existentialists include German philosopher Friedrich Nietzsche and Russian novelist Fyodor Dostoevsky. Whilst their ideas differed in some ways, what connected them was a shared rejection of traditional academic philosophies, considered too remote from actual, authentic experience.

The twentieth-century German philosopher Martin Heidegger was a particular influence on Sartre. During his spell as a POW, Sartre read Heidegger's magnum opus, *Being and Time*, and claimed that it set him on his own philosophical journey. Hence, the similar title for the Existentialist treatise he himself published in 1943: *Being and Nothingness*.

Albert Camus had a very different early life to Sartre and de Beauvoir, being born into an impoverished family in French colonial Algeria. This writer, who would go on to win the Nobel Prize in Literature, had an illiterate widowed mother, and as a teenager had developed tuberculosis. But Camus worked hard to become educated and studied philosophy at the University of Algiers, afterwards working in the theatre and in journalism, and beginning to publish books. Having moved to Paris in 1940, he worked on his novella *L'Étranger* (*The Outsider* or *The Stranger*) and a philosophical essay *Le Mythe de Sisyphe* (*The Myth of Sisyphus*). When the Germans occupied France, he joined the Resistance, writing articles for *Combat*, the clandestine anti-Nazi newspaper he edited.

L'Étranger and *Le Mythe de Sisyphe* were published in 1942 and by the end of the war Camus was celebrated both for his role in the Resistance and for his philosophical writing. Often categorised as an Existentialist, he rejected the label, considering his work to belong instead to the 'absurdist' school of philosophy. Absurdism he defined as the futility of a search for meaning in an incomprehensible universe devoid of meaning and of God – it was the tension between our desire for order, happiness and answers, and the refusal of an indifferent universe to provide them. The theme struck a chord with a population that had just experienced the slaughter, terror and suffering of the war.

Jazz and the muse

The Café de Flore was the epicentre of intellectual and artistic life in post-war Paris, attracting young poets, musicians and jazz lovers. As jazz had been prohibited under the Nazis, the newly liberated French were eager to lap up the musical genre associated

Friends and lovers – Juliette Gréco and Miles Davis in post-war Paris.

with America – and especially with black Americans – which they first enjoyed in Paris in the 1920s.

One newcomer to the Flore was the young French singer Juliette Gréco, an archetypal bohemian with a husky voice, who fitted comfortably into this milieu. 'At the Flore people are less ugly than anywhere else,' she observed breezily. Sartre took her under his wing, saying she had 'millions of poems in her voice', and Camus became a good friend (and likely lover). She quickly acquired the soubriquet *la Muse de l'existentialisme*, and became a fashion icon too, starting the trend for long straight hair – the 'drowning victim' look, according to one journalist – and that classic garment of Left Bank intellectuals, the black polo neck sweater. A passionate affair was sparked with the American jazz musician Miles Davis, during his months-long sojourn in Paris in 1949. When Sartre asked Davis why he didn't marry Gréco, he replied: 'Because I love her too much to make her unhappy.' In true bohemian style the couple decided that, despite being based in different countries, they should remain lovers. And that's what they did – alongside their other relationships – until his death in 1991.

Marriage had no appeal for Sartre and de Beauvoir either. But their rejection of the bourgeois institution was philosophical – tied to their existential concepts of people being free to live 'authentically', giving their life meaning in any way they chose. Whilst devoted to each other, they both took many lovers (for de Beauvoir both men and women), and never lived together. As for Camus, married to his second wife Francine, he too had many affairs and liked spending his nights at the Flore, drinking with the Existentialist crowd and chasing pretty young women. The café had become as much a focal point of adulterous liaisons as of literary talk and philosophising.

The comely young Sonia Brownell, editorial assistant on Cyril Connolly's literary magazine *Horizon* and confirmed Francophile, turned up at the Flore keen to savour the delights of post-war Paris. In 1946, *Horizon* published a French issue denouncing the 'lassitude, brain fatigue, apathy and humdrummery of English writers' and praising the 'intellectual vitality and confidence' of the authors across the Channel. So she left London in order to see it for herself. She hobnobbed with Sartre and Camus, and had an affair with Maurice Merleau-Ponty, editor of the leftist magazine *Les Temps Modernes*, which he had founded with Sartre and de Beauvoir. He was a philosopher too, of the phenomenologist school (i.e. the study of phenomena, or things as they appear in our consciousness, as opposed to reality). But Brownell was less interested in the gobbledygook of phenomenology than in whether or not her lover would leave his wife for her … she was devastated when he didn't.

A few years later, Brownell got married herself, to George Orwell, tying the knot with him on his deathbed. It was a perfunctory, unromantic pairing, but after his death three months later, she realised she'd had genuine feelings for him and missed him greatly. Until her own death in London at the age of 62, she remained Orwell's devoted literary executor and protector of his legacy.

Existentialism was definitely in vogue in Paris during that period. In May 1947, the Paris newspaper *Samedi-Soir* ran a tongue-in-cheek feature on the 'existentialists' timetable', setting out their daily routine: from 11 a.m. to 1 p.m. at the Café de Flore, then lunch at Les Assassins, and the evening at the Bar Vert or the Tabou. The piece was illustrated by a photo of Juliette Gréco and budding screenwriter Roger Vadim 'engaging in depressing thoughts' outside some dive in Saint-Germaine-des-Prés, where the Existentialists 'now drink, dance, love and sleep'.

The Sartre/de Beauvoir double act didn't impress everyone. When the waspish American author Truman Capote spotted the king and queen of Existentialism in a basement bar favoured by bohemians, he described the 'pasty-hued, pipe-sucking Sartre and his spinsterish moll … propped in a corner like an abandoned pair of ventriloquist's dolls'. Sartre, for his part, derided the famously effete Capote as a 'fairy'.

An escape from discrimination

Towards the end of 1948, a 24-year-old black aspiring writer from Harlem called James Baldwin arrived in Paris with forty dollars in his pocket and speaking no French. Baldwin had good reason to leave his homeland and seek his fortune in France. He was desperate to escape pre-civil rights America where segregation was a daily ordeal for the black population, and as a gay man, he had a second form of discrimination to worry about.

He headed straight to Saint-Germaine-des-Prés, where he was welcomed by his friend and mentor, the black American writer Richard Wright. Author of the acclaimed novel *Native Son*, Wright had settled in Paris two years earlier and was well established in the community of Left Bank intellectuals. Soon Baldwin too was befriended by Sartre, Camus et al., and had found lodgings in a cheap Saint-Germain hotel, the Hôtel Verneuil, home to a motley crew of struggling expat arty types. He later recalled:

> Paris hotels had never heard of central heating or hot baths or showers or clean towels and sheets or ham and eggs. Their attitude towards electricity was demonic – once one had seen what they thought of as wiring one wondered why the city had not, long ago, vanished in flame.

No wonder he took refuge at the Flore, where, perhaps at the suggestion of de Beauvoir or Sartre, he worked on the peaceful first floor, just as they had done earlier. 'As soon as I was out of bed I hopefully took notebook and fountain pen off to the upstairs room of the Flore, where I consumed rather a lot of coffee and, as evening approached, rather a lot of alcohol.' It was where he wrote his semi-autobiographical novel, *Go Tell it on the Mountain*, as well as articles and essays.

Baldwin fell in love with Paris. For the first time in his life, he said, he was treated not as a black man, but simply as a *man*, with the freedom to be himself both privately and as a writer. And he relished the ambience of the neighbourhood in which he became embedded, with its cosmopolitan community of writers, artists and musicians. He could not only dance, sing and socialise at the bars and nightclubs of Saint-Germaine, but also explore his sexuality in ways that would have been almost impossible anywhere else; 'my life, in my own eyes, began during that first year in Paris,' he wrote.

It wasn't long before he met and began a relationship with a 17-year-old Swiss boy called Lucien Happersberger, who had turned up in Paris in search of adventure. During Baldwin's first two years there, they became lovers, the experience inspiring his second novel, *Giovanni's Room*.

Baldwin was following a tradition of black Americans settling in Paris. In the early twentieth century, the boxer and entertainer Eugene Bullard had adopted Paris as his home. At the outbreak of the First World War, he joined the French military and fought with such valour he was awarded the *Croix de Guerre*. After the war, many black GIs decided to stay in France rather than return to an America still rife with racism. Later on, black American artists such as Löis Mailou Jones headed to Paris for inspiration and to develop their art more freely. But the most famous black American Parisian was singer-dancer Josephine Baker, one of the biggest stars of the Folies Bergère. She caused a sensation in the 1920s with her risqué *Danse Sauvage*, performed while wearing only a skirt made of a string of artificial bananas. During the Second World War

James Baldwin in Paris, late 1940s.

she helped the French Resistance, afterwards living in a chateau and adopting twelve children of assorted ethnicities to form her 'rainbow tribe'. Sadly, she later went bankrupt, and died in Paris in 1975. But in 2021 she became the first black woman to be honoured with a place at the Panthéon, the mausoleum for France's outstanding historical figures.

Baldwin lived in Paris for nine years before returning to New York. However, it's clear his heart was still in France. In 1970, he uprooted himself again and returned there, moving into a house in the medieval village of Saint-Paul-de-Vence, near Nice. He wrote more books and received famous visitors from America and elsewhere (including Josephine Baker, whose sister lived in Nice) until his death in 1987. The pre-eminent black American intellectual of his era, he broke new ground with his exploration of racial, social and sexual issues in his novels, essays, plays and poetry. His honest portrayal of his personal experiences helped to raise public awareness about prejudice and persecution. As he wisely declared: 'The most dangerous creation of any society is the man who has nothing to lose.'

Their separate ways

The two towering intellects of the post-war Café de Flore, Camus and Sartre, once good friends who discussed philosophy and chased women together, had a high-profile falling out in the 1950s. It was caused by their conflicting political views: Sartre was a defender of the Soviet Union long after the world knew about Stalin's show trials, the purges and the tyranny. But for him political goals came first, and morality second. For Camus it was the opposite. His strongest instinct was humanistic, and morality – political tolerance and civil rights – took precedence. Strongly critical of the totalitarian Soviet Union, he rebuked radical leftists sympathetic to the Soviet model, those, as he put it, 'who call total servitude freedom'. Referring to Sartre and his ilk, he wrote: 'Mistaken ideas always end in bloodshed, but in every case it is someone else's blood. That is why some of our thinkers feel free to say just about anything.'

Camus and Sartre are now both long gone, figures from a vanished age. But the two 'isms' whose birthplace was the Café de Flore are still very much with us. Surrealist art? According to the Paris-based online *Artsper Magazine*, where you can view and buy the work of twenty-first-century Surrealists from various countries:

> Contemporary Surrealism continues to amaze us. Honouring Magritte, Breton and Dalí, the current Surrealists explore in their turn dreams and society. As a true bridge between the dream world, the unconscious and the political struggle, Surrealism transports us. Today it is celebrated through photography, painting and sculpture, offering us an eccentric and mysterious world.

Albert Camus in 1957, the year he won the Nobel Prize.

As for Existentialism and its perennial concerns – identity, freedom, meaning, truth, authenticity – all that 'being and nothingness' business – these too continue to influence many disciplines outside of philosophy, including theology, the theatre, art, literature and psychology. But it's all too easy to get bogged down in endless existential dilemmas. So there is something to be said for the late English writer Colin Wilson's critique of Sartre's philosophy, which he felt had 'found itself in a hole of its own digging'.

Later philosophical developments, wrote Wilson, 'have amounted to walking in circles around that hole'.

The Flore is intent on keeping alive the connection to its illustrious literary past. Since 1994, it has run the annual Prix de Flore literary prize for young authors writing in the French language. The winner receives a prize of several thousand euros and is entitled to a complimentary glass of Pouilly-Fumé at the café every day for a year, with their name engraved on the glass. What style. (Naturally, historic rival the Café les Deux Magots also runs an annual literary prize, the Prix des Deux Magots, established way back in 1933. The winner there also receives a generous cash prize, but no free tipple.)

The quiet upstairs room where Maurras, Sartre, de Beauvoir and Baldwin penned their tomes can also be visited: it's where the ladies' and gents' rooms are situated.

Chapter Eleven

CAFÉ ODEON, ZÜRICH

The Grand Café Odeon opened in 1911, decorated in the fashionable style of Art Nouveau, with high ceilings, large windows, brass panelling, marble-clad walls, and chandeliers. It had its own patisserie in the basement and a billiard room on the first floor. The café was to play a prominent role, in neutral Switzerland, as a haven for noteworthy refugees from the First World War and dictatorship. But that was still a few years away. Before then it was adopted as a favourite haunt by the twentieth century's foremost scientific genius, Albert Einstein, German-born but a Swiss citizen since 1901.

He was living in Zürich and working on his theory of 'general relativity' (the 'special theory of relativity' already under his belt). From 1912 to 1914 he was a professor of theoretical physics at the Federal Institute of Technology (now known as ETH Zürich), not far from the Café Odeon on Limmatquai – at the northern end of Lake Zürich, where it flows into the Limmat River. Einstein didn't merely take his coffee breaks there: he even gave lectures at the café to his students, as he never had more than a handful of them. It was doubtless a more congenial environment for them than an austere classroom, and with refreshments at hand.

Einstein has been so closely associated with the café during that formative period of his life that an anthology of poems called *Einstein at the Odeon Café* was published some years ago in America. In it, the great man is lyrically envisaged sitting there beneath the chandeliers, smoking his cigars and ruminating on the intricacies of space and time.

When he was elected a member of the Prussian Academy of Sciences in Berlin and offered a professorship at a university there without teaching duties, enabling him to concentrate full-time on research, Einstein relocated to the German capital. It was April 1914. A few months later, the First World War broke out, bringing an eclectic crowd of characters to the Café Odeon.

With war raging through most of Europe, there wasn't much room for artistic expression. So it was predictable that peaceful Switzerland, and in particular its largest city, Zürich, would become a beacon for artists, intellectuals and pacifists eager to avoid the violence and chaos engulfing their countries. There they could create so-called 'exile art'.

The mischiefs and madness of Dada

An extraordinary group of exiles arrived in Zürich in 1916 and founded the artistic and literary movement known as Dada. It was anti-war, anti-bourgeois and anarchic, not to mention utterly ludicrous. But it caught on. And so, as well as a refuge from the war, Zürich became the epicentre of the European avant-garde.

One of the originators of Dada was the German poet Hugo Ball, whose *Dada Manifesto* set down his scathing views on the general state of society and on past philosophies that claimed to possess the truth. His ambition was to free poetry from all constraints, in fact to create an entirely new language for it, as the old language was 'doomed' and 'ruined by the filthy hands of capital'. Having made anti-war statements after witnessing Germany's invasion of Belgium, he was deemed a traitor in his country. So he headed for the Swiss border along with his future wife, the cabaret performer Emmy Hennings, settling in Zürich.

Ball and Emmy opened the Cabaret Voltaire in Spiegelgasse, just up the road from the Odeon. Its sole purpose, wrote Ball, was 'to draw attention, across the barriers of war and nationalism, to the few independent spirits who live for other ideals'. The performance and exhibition venue attracted like-minded artists and intellectuals in exile from around Europe, all searching for a new art form that could free people from the madness and brutality of war. It was protest art, experimenting with new kinds of self-expression, using humour, irony and outright craziness.

Ball invented sound poetry, or 'verses without words', and the 'simultaneous poem' in which verses are read out in different languages and at different speeds at the same time. The Dadaists were the first performance artists, the immediate precursors of Surrealism and forerunners of today's 'slam poets'. In Zürich during the years of the First World War, their wacky antics caused an uproar. A favourite gag was to fling open the door of a local tavern and shout 'Dada!' before running off. They also liked to plant outrageous fake stories in the local press, once announcing a spurious duel between two Dadaists at which a popular mawkish poet called J.C. Heer was to be one of the seconds; horrified at being associated with the pranksters, Heer sent the newspaper a furious denial.

Ball's Dada co-founder was the Romanian Tristan Tzara, an experimental poet who became one of the Cabaret Voltaire's star performers. He had arrived in Zürich in 1915 to join his friend and compatriot, the painter Marcel Janco, Like the other Dadaists, they were anti-war, anti-establishment and keen to do something daring and provocative. Janco decorated the Cabaret Voltaire, carved the ferocious, primitive-looking masks worn by performers on stilts, and gave 'hissing concerts' – a concert comprised of hisses, as the name suggests. And together with Tzara and the German poet Richard Hülsenbeck, Janco improvised onomatopoeic simultaneous poems.

The origin of the term Dada has never been fully agreed upon. According to some, it came from the Romanian and Russian word *da*, meaning yes. Others believe it was taken from a baby's first word for 'father'. According to Hülsenbeck, he and Hugo Ball came upon it randomly in a French-German dictionary – it was the French nickname for a hobby horse, which they reckoned fitted the carefree, childlike image of their movement. Janco, however, claimed that his friend Tzara had coined the term.

The Dadaists disagreed about a lot, including what Dada was all about. As Ball put it: 'For us, art is not an end in itself … it is an opportunity for the true perception and criticism of the times we live in.' On the other hand, Tzara, a nihilist at heart, stated: 'Everything is Dada. Beware of Dada. Anti-Dadaism is a disease … man's normal condition is Dada. But the real Dadas are against Dada.' Complete nonsense.

One thing they did agree on was to have their headquarters at the Café Odeon. When they all got together – Tzara and Ball, and Ball's girlfriend Emmy, Marcel Janco, Richard Hülsenbeck, the German sculptor and poet Jean Arp and his Swiss girlfriend, the dancer and artist Sophie Taeuber, the German graphic artist Hans Richter – their table talk was so madcap and incoherent that the café's waiters were left utterly bewildered. But their regular gatherings endowed the place with its enduring reputation as the cradle of Dadaism.

Jean Arp described a typical evening of 'total pandemonium' at the 'gaudy, motley, overcrowded' Cabaret Voltaire:

> Tzara is wiggling his behind like the belly of an Oriental dancer. Janco is playing an invisible violin and bowing and scraping. Madame Hennings, with a Madonna face, is doing the splits. Hülsenbeck is banging away nonstop on the great drum, with Ball accompanying him on the piano, pale as a chalky ghost.

Yet these crazy goings-on struck the Dadaists as no more absurd than the war itself, in which millions were being slaughtered for reasons that were hard to comprehend. Perhaps they had a point.

In the end, Ball and Tzara fell out due to their conflicting objectives. Ball disagreed with Tzara's ambition to turn Dada into an international movement with a systematic doctrine. So he left Zürich in May 1917, with Emmy in tow, and moved to the southern Swiss canton of Ticino, where he devoted himself to mystical Catholicism. Tzara meanwhile continued to stage shows – now at the Galerie Dada on Bahnhofstrasse, as the Cabaret Voltaire had closed down – which usually turned into a riot. He took pleasure in 'letting fly at the bourgeois', according to Hans Richter, thus putting himself at permanent odds with the Swiss authorities. Tzara also composed his own, more comprehensive *Dada Manifesto*, spreading his anarchic message successfully to artists far and wide. As a result, Dada groups sprang up in Berlin, Hamburg, Paris and even New York.

But Surrealism was hot on Dada's heels and the movement fizzled out in the early post-war years, with many Dadaists decamping to the Surrealist movement.

Dadaist pals in Zürich during the First World War: Jean Arp, Tristan Tzara and Hans Richter.

In 1919, Tzara himself, the self-styled 'president of Dada', moved to Paris, joining the staff of André Breton's *Littérature* magazine. He wrote his Dadaist plays, *The Gas Heart* and *Handkerchief of Clouds*, but eventually Tzara too gave in and aligned himself with Breton's Surrealism.

James Joyce gets into a row …

The carry-ons of a clutch of exiled personalities in Zürich during the First World War was exactly what, a half-century later, fired the imagination of playwright Tom Stoppard. His play *Travesties*, first staged in London by the Royal Shakespeare Company in 1974, revolves around the real-life figure of Henry Carr, a low-level diplomat at the British consulate in Zürich during that period. In the play, the now elderly Carr reminisces about his dealings with three exiles then living in the city: Tristan Tzara, Irish writer James Joyce and Comrade Vladimir Ilyich Ulyanov, better known as Lenin.

The riotous Tzara would have been hard to avoid in Zürich. And Carr no doubt encountered Lenin at the Café Odeon, because when not studying books at the central library, the Bolshevik revolutionary spent much of his time there, poring over the six daily editions of the *Neue Zürcher Zeitung*, holding court with other exiled Russian communists and plotting to take over the world. Lenin's dingy rented flat on Spiegelgasse (diagonally across the street from the Cabaret Voltaire) would never have sufficed for such meetings. It overlooked a smelly sausage factory, and he and his wife Nadya couldn't even open a window.

Joyce too could be seen at the café; it was where he often went to work on his stream-of-consciousness novel *Ulysses*. But Carr became acquainted with the writer via other means. Joyce was co-founder of a theatre company called the English Players, which had been pitched to the British government as a contribution to the war effort, and he became its business manager. It staged works mainly by Irish playwrights. The company asked Carr whether he'd like to appear in its production of Oscar Wilde's *The Importance of Being Earnest*, and the consular official readily agreed. He was duly cast in the starring role of Algernon Moncrieff.

By all accounts, Carr, a keen thespian, performed well in the role, but afterwards became embroiled in a dispute over his fee with Joyce. As an amateur actor, Carr was paid only a modest ten francs, but due to his enthusiasm for donning the

James Joyce in Zürich, *c.*1915.

proper theatrical costume, he had shelled out for new trousers, hat and gloves for his appearance as Algernon, and now demanded reimbursement. Joyce refused, instead demanding that Carr pay for the five complimentary tickets he had been given and then sold to friends. He also accused Carr of slandering him. In the end, the matter was settled in court with the judge deciding in favour of Joyce regarding the slander, but in favour of Carr regarding the reimbursement. Joyce later had his revenge: an episode in *Ulysses* lampoons Carr as a foul-mouthed drunk.

Stoppard based his play on this real-life historical vignette, using it to explore the themes of war and revolution, art and theatre, meaning and nonsense. He inserts characters and plot elements from *The Importance of Being Earnest*, employs linguistic devices such as limericks and puns, and introduces a running vaudeville motif. It was regarded as a comic masterpiece.

In Act II of *Travesties*, Henry Carr remarks:

> I learned three things in Zürich during the war … Firstly, you're either a revolutionary or you're not, and if you're not you might as well be an artist as anything else. Secondly, if you can't be an artist, you might as well be a revolutionary … I forget the third thing.

Which sums up rather well the mood in Zürich during the First World War.

Quite a few theatrical productions could have been inspired by the interplay of Zürich's vibrant hodgepodge of expats during that period. Joyce had opted for self-imposed exile from his native Ireland in 1904, feeling himself constricted there – he disdained the unhealthily close relationship between the Catholic Church and the Irish state – and had been living mostly in Trieste. He and his future wife, Nora Barnacle, arrived in Zürich in 1915 to find a city 'crowded with refugees'. The environment suited him perfectly. He felt that the air of experimentation, as embodied by the Dadaists, was conducive to his writing of *Ulysses*. He also savoured the cosmopolitan ambience at the city's literary cafés, especially the Odeon, where he befriended another exile, Austrian novelist Stefan Zweig, who was no doubt pining away for his beloved Café Central in Vienna. After all, the Central was exactly the sort of traditional European coffee house on which the Odeon was modelled. Zweig evidently approved of the radically modernist Joyce; he went on to organise the premiere of Joyce's play *Exiles* in Munich after the war.

… while Lenin plots a revolution

It was at the Odeon that Joyce reputedly met Lenin on at least one occasion. But if the Russian agitator tried to rile up the Irishman against Ireland's old adversary, the British, he didn't succeed; Joyce was staying strictly apolitical there, focusing purely on his literary work. Lenin tried not to attract the attention of the police, as he didn't want to be deported, but on the sly advocated armed insurrection in Switzerland. He didn't believe in pacifism or neutrality, declaring: 'The neutrality of Switzerland is a bourgeois fraud and means submission to the imperialist war.' Zweig, who had fled to Zürich precisely because of his pacifist beliefs, observed Lenin at the Odeon from time to time. How, Zweig wondered after the momentous Russian Revolution, had this 'obstinate little man' ever become so important?

Tristan Tzara, in later life, claimed to have played chess and 'exchanged ideas' with Lenin, but it sounds unlikely. Why would the grave-minded Lenin have consorted with an anarchic jokester like Tzara? The Dadaist Hans Richter recalled seeing Lenin at the library and once hearing him speak at a political meeting; he'd been impressed by the Russian's fluent German. The Swiss authorities, Richter observed, seemed much more suspicious of the Dadaist crowd than they were of the 'quiet, studious Russians'. They obviously felt the Dadaists 'were capable of perpetrating some new enormity at any moment', whilst the unostentatious Russians were 'merely planning world revolution'.

The Swiss police had a tough job trying to keep tabs on all the bohemians, radicals and other unconventional types in their country at that time. To make matters worse, Switzerland was swarming with spies. Some were officials at the embassies of the belligerent nations, others were ordinary civilians co-opted into spying duties: waiters and waitresses, hotel staff and shop workers, paid to watch and listen to persons of interest, eavesdropping on conversations, digging around in wastepaper baskets, reporting back on findings.

The legendary exotic dancer and spy Mata Hari (real name Margaretha Zelle) spent some time in Zürich in 1915. She was Dutch, and given Holland's neutrality during the war, could cross borders freely. During her stay in the city, the sultry seductress danced in a cabaret show on the first floor of the Café Odeon. Two years later, aged 41, she was convicted of spying for Germany (without evidence and pleading her innocence) and executed by a firing squad of French soldiers. According to reporter Henry Wales of the International News Service, who witnessed the event, she refused a blindfold, gazed straight ahead and 'did not move a muscle'. Real style, right to the end.

Zürich still hangs on to its fleeting brush with the immortal spy, boasting a trendy Mata Hari cocktail bar with plush red seating, mood lighting and rock music – perhaps the millennials' highest form of tribute.

Lenin's attempts to use the 'imperialist war' as a catalyst for an armed uprising against capitalism failed dismally in Switzerland. Both in Bern and in Zürich his radical ideas fell on deaf ears and the left-wingers who gathered around him rejected his hard political line. By March 1917, disillusioned with the neutral Swiss and hearing of early stirrings of revolution in Russia, he resolved to return to St Petersburg. Receiving permission to travel by train across Germany (with which Russia was at war), in April he left Switzerland for good. Six months later,

Mata Hari in her sultry heyday.

the October Revolution broke out, the Bolsheviks seized control and Lenin secured his place in history.

Aleksandr Solzhenitsyn's book *Lenin in Zürich*, first published in the West in the 1970s, shows the communist agitator stewing in Switzerland during the First World War, a humourless obsessive, chronically frustrated by financial concerns and the deeply divided socialist movement. However, Lenin did have something to show for his stay in the city, having written a short book with a snappy title: *Imperialism, the Highest Stage of Capitalism*; it was published in Russia shortly after his return to the country.

James Joyce and Nora Barnacle didn't stay in Zürich for long after the war. The city had become more expensive, and with its émigré population returning home, he felt increasingly isolated. The couple departed Zürich in October 1919 and by the following summer were living in Paris. In 1922, *Ulysses* was published in Paris by Sylvia Beach of the fabled Shakespeare and Company bookstore, but it would be several years before its publication in the UK or America, where it was banned as obscene. Joyce at last married Nora in 1931 and Paris remained their primary residence. But they travelled frequently, especially to Switzerland, where Joyce sought medical treatment for his worsening eye problems and psychiatric help for his daughter Lucia, who had been diagnosed with schizophrenia.

After the fall of France in 1940, neutral Switzerland was once more a wartime refuge for Joyce and his family, and they returned to Zürich. The writer died there only a year later, following surgery for a perforated ulcer.

The Odeon had a chequered history during the later decades of the twentieth century. In the early 1970s it was taken over by an unruly, druggy young crowd, the café was trashed, and as a result, the police closed it down. But the city listed the building as a protected monument and in 1972 it was acquired by the restaurateur Fred Tschanz, who renovated and reopened it, albeit reduced in size, with part of the former café becoming a pharmacy. It still had a somewhat dodgy reputation, but the shrewd Tschanz managed to replace its 'rocker and drug scene' customers with members of Zürich's respectable, well-heeled gay community, luring them away from other gay watering holes. What's more, he ensured the venue's security by striking a deal with the local Hells Angels, who agreed to keep troublemakers out. Genius.

Lenin, quietly plotting world revolution in Zürich in 1916.

Zürich's Café Odeon, 1959.

The present-day Café Bar Odeon is not far from what it was at its launch a century ago: an Art Nouveau gem inspired by the coffee house culture of Habsburg-era Vienna. But there's one big difference now, explains its manager: 'Today we can no longer live from a coffee table that is occupied for three to four hours.' Poets and other bohemians take note …

Chapter Twelve

CAFÉ LUITPOLD, MUNICH

Within Germany, the Bavarians have a lifestyle all their own. They are a jovial, beer-swilling lot in their emblematic lederhosen, dirndls, and feathered Tyrolean hats. So different to the Prussians to the north, with their reputation for being stiff-necked and humourless. Famous for their cavernous beer halls, beer gardens and, in the state capital of Munich, the annual Oktoberfest – the world's biggest beer festival, dating back to the early nineteenth century – you might think the Bavarians weren't particularly fussed about café culture. But you'd be wrong. Despite its unique traits, Munich is a quintessential central European city with its own fair share of historic cafés. The bombs of the Second World War, financial misfortune, changes of ownership and the simple passing of time have put paid to most of them, but left us with the last great survivor: Café Luitpold, opened in 1888.

It was named after Prince Regent Luitpold of Bavaria's Wittelsbach dynasty, who ruled in place of his mentally unstable nephew, King Ludwig II, aka Mad King Ludwig. Luitpold had begun his regency two years earlier and soon won public approval. Bavaria became the most democratically governed kingdom in Germany and the period of Luitpold's regency would be regarded as a golden age for the region and its cultural centre, Munich.

The café named in his honour was built on Briennerstrasse, a short stroll from Luitpold's home at the Residenz, the Wittelsbach royal palace. Modelled on the grand cafés of the Austro-Hungarian Empire, the 'coffee palace' was designed in an extravagant blend of styles: Neo-Renaissance, Neo-Baroque, Neo-Rococo. One of Europe's largest cafés when it opened, it could seat up to 2,000 and had some twenty rooms and lounges, including a palm garden, dance hall, and the biggest billiard hall in the German Empire, with fourteen billiard tables. There was a richly decorated main hall with a soaring, lavishly painted dome and thirty-eight black marble columns, a hall of mirrors, wall paintings, fountains, sculptures and bronze ornamentation. What's more, it was one of the first public buildings in the city to be lit by electricity – a thrilling novelty. Members of the royal family graced it with their presence, aristocrats flocked to it, as did the ordinary folk of Munich – everyone from cash-strapped students to well-heeled professionals.

The great columned hall of Munich's Café Luitpold when it opened in 1888.

The Café Luitpold, Munich, at the turn of the twentieth century.

The Café Luitpold's first association with artists came through the landscape painter Hugo Bürgel, a member of the Munich Artists' Cooperative. Dissatisfied with the standard and old-fashioned style of painting represented by the cooperative, he founded the spin-off Luitpold Group, which advocated a more modern approach to art. The writers were not far behind – in 1896, publisher Albert Langen launched his weekly satirical magazine *Simplicissimus* (Latin for 'the simplest') from a room at the café. It featured articles by the top-ranking writers of the day, including Thomas Mann, Frank Wedekind, Hermann Hesse, Rainer Maria Rilke, and Erich Kästner, author of the children's classic *Emil and the Detectives*. The magazine poked fun at the stolid Prussians and their militarism, and ridiculed rigid German social and class distinctions from the viewpoint of Munich's more relaxed, liberal atmosphere. *Simplicissimus* was a long-lasting publication, folding only in 1967.

The women speak up

The café played another, even more important role, as a site closely connected to the emancipation of women in Bavaria, and not just by offering waitresses and other female staff better working conditions than other venues. In October 1899, the café's sumptuous ballroom also hosted the first Bavarian Women's Day. Several women gave speeches on the ideals and goals of the women's movement, placing special emphasis on women's education; at the time they were not admitted to German universities. In 1903, under the direction of the Prince Regent, women were at last accorded equal rights to study, attend lectures and gain degrees at all universities in Bavaria. Luitpold knew only too well that this was now overdue. After all, years earlier his own daughter, Princess Therese, had been the first woman to receive an honorary doctorate from Munich's Ludwig Maximilian University. A distinguished ethnologist and scientist in zoology and botany, Therese was an honorary member of the Bavarian Academy of Sciences and Humanities. There is even a species of Peruvian lizard, *Microlophus theresiae*, named in her honour. What further proof was needed of the value of education to the 'fair sex'?

Blue Riders

A second, highly significant connection between the café and the art world was established early in the twentieth century with a band of experimental artists who would achieve fame as Der Blaue Reiter, the Blue Rider group. Its leading light was Wassily Kandinsky, a Russian artist who had arrived in Munich in 1896 to study at its Academy of Fine Arts. In 1909 he joined the Neue Künstlervereinigung München (New Artists' Association of Munich), proponents of the Expressionist school. He became its first president and exhibited work with them. But he found them too conservative for his taste; Kandinsky was an artistic theorist with a more radical vision. When the association insisted he abandon his abstract style and produce more 'understandable' works, he resigned.

In 1911 – the year the Prince Regent held his ninetieth birthday celebration at the café which bore his name – Kandinsky formed his own artistic offshoot, together with Munich-born painter and printmaker Franz Marc and other artists, including the Berliner Gabriele Münter, his talented protégé and lover. He named it Der Blaue Reiter after his painting of the same name, which depicts a small horseback figure in a blue cloak galloping through a meadow. The movement came into being at the maverick artists' favoured retreat, the Café Luitpold – an expedient choice, as the building complex housing the café, the Luitpoldblock, was also home to the Hans Goltz art dealership and gallery. Goltz was a champion of modernism in art and had every sympathy with the cutting-edge work of Kandinsky and his friends.

The Swiss-born experimental artist Paul Klee met Kandinsky at the Luitpold in late 1911 and they formed an immediate bond. Klee, the younger of the two by thirteen years, said Kandinsky had 'an exceptionally beautiful and lucid mind'. Kandinsky in turn summed up his impression of his fellow artist with the words: 'What depth of soul!' Klee allied himself with the Blue Rider group and joined the editorial team of the *Blue Rider Almanac* founded by Kandinsky and Marc; its first edition was published in May 1912. Klee's individualistic style was influenced not only by Expressionism, but also by Surrealism and Cubism, the movements cross-pollinating in his work.

The Blue Rider artists held two exhibitions in Munich. The second one, in 1912, was held at the Hans Goltz gallery and called *Schwarz-Weiß* (Black-White), because it comprised etchings, drawings, lithographs and woodcuts, all of them in those two colours. Some 300 works by Kandinsky, Klee and others were put on show. Travelling exhibitions in other German cities and elsewhere in Europe followed.

Kandinsky's paintings – large and colourful freeform works – didn't attempt to represent the exterior world, but rather to express the 'inner feelings of the soul'; they were a reflection of what you felt, not what you saw. In *The Blue Rider Almanac* and his treatise *On the Spiritual in Art* he defended and promoted abstract art, claiming that all forms of art were able to convey some level of spirituality. And he believed that colour could be used in a painting as an autonomous entity and not just as a visual description of something. The colour blue in particular had a spiritual significance for him, as he believed it represented infinity. Kandinsky's ideas made a big impact on the art world in England, where his treatise was translated into English and reviewed in the periodical *Art News*.

His colleague Marc's work mostly portrayed animals in nature, using bright primary colours in an almost cubist style. The paintings were simple yet imbued with feeling, with different colours for different emotions – blue was used to portray masculinity and spirituality, yellow represented feminine joy, and red denoted violence. His pictures began to attract serious attention in influential artistic circles.

The Blue Rider artists were important pioneers of modern art in the twentieth century, part of the wider school of German Expressionism. But their circle was to be short-lived. At the outbreak of the First World War, it was inevitably forced to disband. Kandinsky made his way back to Russia via Switzerland and Sweden. Marc meanwhile was drafted into the Imperial German Army as a cavalryman and by early 1916 was working in the field of military camouflage, painting canvas covers to hide artillery from aerial observation. In a letter to his wife, he explained that he painted nine such tarpaulin covers in a variety of styles, 'from Manet to Kandinsky'. The German government identified a number of distinguished artists to be withdrawn from combat for their own safety, and Marc was on the list. However, within a few months he was at the front and engaged in the Battle of Verdun. Before orders for his reassignment could reach him, he was killed when his head was struck by flying shrapnel.

That same month, Klee was conscripted as a *Landsturmsoldat* (a soldier in the German reserve forces). He was deeply affected by the death of his friends Franz Marc and August Macke, another Blue Rider artist killed early in the war, aged 27. Klee gave vent to his sorrow by creating pen and ink lithographs on war themes. More fortunate than the other two, he did make it to a safe job behind the front. He was moved to an aircraft maintenance company, where he performed skilled manual tasks such as restoring aircraft camouflage. In 1917 he was transferred to the Royal Bavarian Flying School in Gersthofen, north-west of Munich, to work as a clerk, and allowed to continue painting there throughout the war, even to exhibit in several shows. His work sold well and he was hailed by critics as the pre-eminent new German artist.

The fertile ground of the Weimar Republic

In post-Revolution Russia, Kandinsky got involved in the new communist regime's cultural politics, collaborating in art education and museum reform, teaching art and becoming the first director of Moscow's Institute of Artistic Culture. But inevitably, his style of spiritual expressionism in art was deemed too bourgeois, personal and idiosyncratic for the Bolsheviks. If he'd stayed on he might easily have ended up in a Siberian labour camp or been shot. Luckily, in 1921 he accepted an invitation to teach at the Bauhaus school of art and architecture in the central German city of Weimar, established three years earlier by the architect Walter Gropius. Kandinsky's friend Paul Klee was already there, teaching in the bookbinding, stained glass and mural painting workshops.

The aim of the Bauhaus school was to merge the fine arts with technical skills and crafts such as carpentry, metalworking and typography, graphic art, pottery, weaving and photography. It was a marriage of functionality and aesthetics. Klee welcomed the many conflicting theories and opinions within the Bauhaus, commenting: 'I approve of these forces competing with one another if the result is achievement.' The first Bauhaus exhibition and festival was held in 1922.

A year later, Kandinsky and Klee formed a new artistic unit together with two other former members of the Blue Rider set, the German-American painter Lyonel Feininger

Paul Klee (left) and Wassily Kandinsky in their Bauhaus years, late 1920s.

and Russian painter Alexej von Jawlensky. They called it Die Blaue Vier (The Blue Four), showing that they hadn't really left behind the inspired, trailblazing movement launched at the Café Luitpold more than a decade earlier. The Blue Four went on to lecture and mount successful exhibitions of their work in Europe and America.

In the early 1920s, German Expressionism was superseded by Bauhaus, and by the Neue Sachlichkeit (New Objectivity) school of art which emerged in response to the cataclysm of the First World War. The movement was satirical, cynical, a form of ruthless social commentary; two of its chief exponents were Otto Dix and George Grosz. Add to this the emergence of the austere movement known as Constructivism – a geometric reflection of the industrial world – and it's clear the Weimar Republic was fertile ground for experimental art. Not only in painting and drawing, but in cinema too, where German Expressionism continued to flourish with films such as F.W. Murnau's 1922 *Nosferatu* and Fritz Lang's 1927 *Metropolis*.

Indeed, the creative arts were both innovative and exciting during the Weimar period … until the arrival of the Nazis, who condemned it all as 'degenerate'.

Don't fool yourself, Schicklgruber

Adolf Hitler loved Munich. He said it was the city closest to his heart. It's certainly the one that will forever be most closely linked with him.

There are many reasons for this. Whilst Berlin was the powerful seat of his empire and Nuremberg the site of the annual rallies, which were his greatest propaganda events, it was in Munich that things really took off for him. The first German city he went to on leaving Austria as a young man, it was also where he went back to after serving in the First World War. Munich was where he joined and then took over a paltry little far-right political outfit and turned it into the Nazi Party. Finally, it was the city where, if Hitler can be said to have had any genuine romantic or sexual responses to females, he first acted upon them, through unconventional relationships with his ill-fated niece Geli Raubal and his equally doomed 'secret mistress', Eva Braun.

In the early years after the First World War (once the brief Munich Soviet Republic of 1919 was overthrown), Hitler embedded himself in the city's turbulent political scene, swiftly gaining a reputation as an effective demagogue. He'd discovered what he was best at: inciting discontent, fanning anti-Semitism and provoking violence. Most of this was done at Munich's boisterous beer halls, where the combination of beer drinking and demagoguery was a popular mix. Hitler understood the crowds and knew how to manipulate them. But though he spent many hours at beer halls stirring up trouble, he wasn't a big drinker himself, and in time would become teetotal.

By 1921 he was heading the growing Nationalsozialistische Deutsche Arbeiterpartei (National Socialist German Workers' Party), the Nazi Party for short. Hitler felt totally at home in Munich. He soon lit upon a café that for the next couple of years would serve as a regular meeting place for the assorted malcontents and misfits, embittered war veterans and would-be revolutionaries he gathered around him. This was the Café Neumayr behind St Peter's Church, by the open air food market known as the Viktualienmarkt. A table was reserved for him there every Monday evening, for discussions during which he would try out new ideas on his cronies.

He also gave occasional speeches at the Neumayr, one of which was attended by First World War flying ace Hermann Göring, who had come along to check out the leader of the new National Socialist Party. As Hitler expounded on the Nazi route to power, insisting that brute force was needed to back up their threats, Göring sat inconspicuously in the background. As he later recounted: 'That was what I wanted to hear. He wanted to build up a party that would make Germany strong and smash the Treaty of Versailles. "Well," I said to myself, "that's the party for me!"' Hitler was delighted to welcome into the fold the recipient of the *Pour le Mérite* – aka the Blue Max – Germany's highest medal for valour. He recognised the propaganda value.

In the failed Beer Hall Putsch, which followed on 9 November 1923, Göring was shot in the groin but managed to flee the country, his painful injury turning him into a morphine addict. Meanwhile, Hitler's arrest and conviction for treason landed him with a cushy nine-month stint at Landsberg Prison, during which he dictated *Mein Kampf* to an admiring Rudolf Hess. Afterwards, with the re-establishment of the Nazi

Party in 1925, Hitler settled into the existence of a less overtly rabble-rousing Munich politician. He realised he would have to use the democratic system afforded by the Weimar Republic to gain power (before abolishing that democracy, of course).

There were congenial daily routines for Hitler in his favourite city. Years before he became a vegetarian, he picked out his favourite restaurants. First there was the Schelling-Salon, a pleasant, airy eatery, at the time done up in the style of a Viennese coffee house (which perhaps was what drew him to it). He liked lunching there with his associates, but when the owner cut off his credit due to unpaid bills he switched his allegiance to the Osteria Bavaria (today called the Osteria Italiana). The first restaurant in Munich to specialise in Italian cuisine, it was a hangout of artists and students from the Academy of Fine Arts – an ambience that no doubt appealed to the one-time aspiring painter.

Both establishments were on Schellingstrasse in the heart of Schwabing, a district adjacent to the city centre and renowned as Munich's bohemian quarter. Now it became the Nazis' main stamping ground as well. It was on Schellingstrasse that the party had its headquarters from 1925 to 1931, in the same building as the studio of Hitler's official photographer, Heinrich Hoffman. The offices of the party's official newspaper, the rabidly anti-Semitic *Völkischer Beobachter* (the *People's Observer*), were also on this street.

As for cafés, he now consigned the Neumayr to the past and plumped for somewhere in more upscale surroundings, where he could recreate the café culture from his pre-war Vienna days. He chose the Café Heck on the corner of Ludwigstrasse and Galeriestrasse, just off the Odeonsplatz with its Field Marshals' Hall (where his putsch had come to a sticky end). The café's handsome building backed on to the pleasant Hofgarten, where in good weather Hitler would sit with his fellow Nazis at an outdoor table under the trees.

By the late 1920s, he had become quite a celebrity and stopped going to the Heck, as he was pestered by too many people stopping at his table for a chat, to shake his hand or ask for his autograph. He no longer felt comfortable mingling with the general public in an informal, unchoreographed manner. The writer Klaus Mann, son of Thomas, captured this period of Hitler's life in his later recollections. The Mann family was resident in Munich and Klaus had once been a regular at the Café Luitpold. But in the early 1930s he began avoiding it because 'it had become the meeting place of the SA and the SS; a decent person no longer frequented it'. Klaus Mann wrote that the Führer himself must have had an aversion to mingling with 'his brave men', because instead of the Luitpold he patronised the more sedate Carlton Tea Room, on the opposite side of Briennerstrasse. As Mann recalled in his 1942 autobiography, *The Turning Point*:

> It was at the beginning of 1932 that I spent half-an-hour or so watching [Hitler] at a table just a few feet from mine. The Carlton Tea Room in

Hitler with his Nazi cronies at the Café Heck in Munich, 1929.

Munich's Café Luitpold in 1930, before it was overrun by Nazis.

> Munich was one of his favourite places. … I found him surprisingly ugly, much more vulgar than I had anticipated. … He was flabby and foul and without any marks of greatness, a frustrated, hysterical petty bourgeois. It was a most unpleasant experience to have him so close to me, but at the same time it meant something like a relief. For I was positive that he had no chance to conquer Germany. 'He is not to be our dictator,' I felt with a sort of malignant satisfaction. 'You have no chance, silly little moustache. Don't fool yourself, Schicklgruber: you are a washout. Five years from now, nobody will remember your name.'

Mann chided himself for not having seen 'the writing on the wall' that day at the Carlton Tea Room. Like many others, he underestimated the power that 'silly little moustache' would one day wield.

Late-night summons to the café

Once he came to power in 1933, Hitler moved to Berlin and lived at the Reich Chancellery, but he didn't lose his affection for Munich – the cradle of his movement – and returned often. He would stay at his luxury eight-room apartment at Prinzregentenplatz, to the east of the Isar River, which he retained until the end.

Hitler's architect, Albert Speer, also recorded his boss's café-visiting habits in his memoirs, *Inside the Third Reich*:

> He frequently visited Carlton's Tearoom, a bogus luxurious place with reproduction furniture and fake crystal chandeliers. He liked it because the people there left him undisturbed, did not bother him with applause or requests for autographs, as was generally the case elsewhere in Munich.
>
> Frequently I would receive a telephone call late at night from Hitler's apartment: 'The Führer is driving over to the Café Heck and has asked that you come too.' I would have to get out of bed and had no prospect of returning before two or three o'clock in the morning.
>
> Occasionally Hitler would apologise. 'I formed the habit of staying up late during our days of struggle. After rallies I would have to sit down with the old fighters, and besides my speeches usually stirred me up so much that I would not have been able to sleep before early morning.'
>
> The Café Heck, in contrast to Carlton's Tearoom, was furnished with plain wooden chairs and iron tables. It was the old party café where Hitler used to meet his comrades. But any such meetings stopped after 1933. The Munich group had shown him so much devotion over so many years that I had expected him to have a group of close Munich friends; but there was nothing of the sort. On the contrary, Hitler tended to become sulky when one of the old comrades wanted to speak to him, and almost always managed to refuse such requests … no doubt the old party comrades did not always assume the tone of respectful distance that Hitler … now thought proper.

Hitler instructs the masses on good and bad art

As soon as he came to power Hitler launched into his grandiose architectural projects for Munich by laying the cornerstone for the Haus der Deutschen Kunst, the House of German Art, to be sited at the southern end of the Englischer Garten. This was a big deal for Hitler, as he had proclaimed Munich to be the 'capital city of German art', so the SS, the SA (the thuggish Brownshirts) and the Hitler Youth boys all paraded in celebration of this major cultural event, on 15 October 1933. When Hitler struck the cornerstone with a silver hammer, the hammer broke. An ill omen, as it turned out: the building's architect, Paul Ludwig Troost, fell ill and died three months later.

The art museum's heralded opening took place in the summer of 1937. A monolithic edifice fronted by a long row of Greek-style columns, it led some to mock it as 'Athens Central Train Station'. The inaugural exhibition, attended by the Führer and all the Nazi bigwigs, was the Grosse Deutsche Kunstausstellung (Great German Art Exhibition). On display were works complying with the 'National Socialist understanding of German art', the only kind officially endorsed. They took their cue from the classical art of the Greeks and Romans, with their depictions of romantic and heroic themes. Crucially, they had to be easily understood by the average citizen.

This was all in total contrast to the 'disgusting and worthless' stuff on show concurrently at the exhibition of Entartete Kunst or Degenerate Art. That was put on at a much more modest venue on Galeriestrasse, a few steps from the Café Heck. German museums had been purged of 650 avant-garde works branded degenerate because, as Hitler put it in a speech, they 'insult German feeling, or destroy or confuse natural form or simply reveal an absence of adequate manual and artistic skill'. He declared war on these 'dilettantes and art swindlers'.

Works by Kandinsky and Klee, George Grosz, Otto Dix, Oskar Kokoschka and Marc Chagall were included in the degenerate roundup. Propaganda minister Josef Goebbels later ordered a more thorough scouring of German art collections, bringing the total number of works seized by the Nazis to more than 16,000. Many were sold, many others destroyed.

Kandinsky and Klee had both left Germany the year the Nazis came to power. The Bauhaus school, where Kandinsky had still been teaching, was shut by the Nazis, and Klee was fired from his teaching post at the Düsseldorf Academy of Fine Arts. So the Klee family left for Switzerland, whilst Kandinsky settled in Paris. There the Blue Rider trailblazers continued to work until they contracted illnesses and died during the Second World War, Kandinsky at the age of 78 and Klee at 60.

Rescued by a woman

The Lenbachhaus is a world-class art museum in Munich, most famous for its extensive collection of works by the Blue Rider artists. For this it has Kandinsky's devoted lover, the artist Gabriele Münter, to thank. They were together for a decade before Kandinsky returned to Russia alone in 1914. There he met his future wife, Nina, and so his relationship with Münter ended. The split affected her deeply and she didn't pick up a paintbrush for nearly ten years. 'In the eyes of many,' she remarked dolefully, 'I was only an unnecessary side-dish to Kandinsky.'

By the 1930s, Münter was living in the Bavarian market town of Murnau. As the Nazis came to power and condemned modernist art movements, she had her own artwork, as well as a great deal of the works produced by Kandinsky and the other Blue Rider members, hastily gathered up and transported to her house, where she hid them. Despite several searches of the property by the Nazi authorities, they were never found.

German Expressionist painter Gabriele Münter in a portrait by Wassily Kandinsky, 1905.

On her eightieth birthday in 1957, Münter donated more than a thousand Blue Rider works to the Lenbachhaus museum. She died five years later, but her invaluable legacy lives on.

As for the Café Luitpold, like most of Munich it was severely damaged in the bombing towards the end of the Second World War. It reopened in a simplified form in 1948, and later underwent a series of makeovers. At last, an extensive renovation in 2010 returned the historic café to its former glory, including the glass-domed inner courtyard with palm trees and ornamental pool. Along with the traditional refreshments, it now serves up a range of cultural events – concerts, lectures and discussions with speakers from the arts and sciences. There is also a small museum dedicated to its colourful past, lest we be in danger of forgetting it.

Chapter Thirteen

GRAN CAFÉ DE GIJÓN, MADRID

Spain's premier literary café opened its doors on the principal boulevard of central Madrid, the Paseo de Recoletos, in 1888. The owner, Don Gumersindo García, named his business after the city of his birth in the north-western province of Asturias. By the close of the nineteenth century, it was attracting the most experimental novelists, poets and philosophers in Spain at the time. Known as the Generation of '98, they had been deeply affected by Spain's humiliating defeat in the Spanish-American War of 1898, and were committed to a cultural renewal allied with modernism.

Gran Café de Gijón, Madrid.

The bloody war against the Americans had resulted in thousands of dead Spaniards and the loss of all of Spain's colonies in the Americas and the Pacific. The country was in a dire political and social state. Whilst the intellectuals of the Generation of '98 often conveyed nostalgia for Spain's past glories and its way of life, they broke with literary tradition to create new forms and techniques. Their writing became more minimalist and dialogue-driven, less descriptive. The most radical among them was the playwright and novelist Ramón del Valle-Inclán. He managed successfully to subvert the early twentieth-century conventions of the Spanish theatre, and his influence was strongly felt by the Spanish dramatists who came after him.

The Café de Gijón was the foremost Madrid coffee house to revive the centuries-old Spanish custom of the *tertulia*, a social gathering to discuss literary matters, politics or current affairs. The word has an interesting etymology. In the sixteenth century, King Philip II of Spain was greatly absorbed by the cultures of the ancient world, and especially the writings of the early Christian author Quintus Septimius Florens Tertullianus. As King Philip gathered together academics and erudite courtiers to discuss these Latin works with him, the name *tertulia* was coined to mean a learned discussion. Its participants are called *contertulios*.

How to lose an arm

Ramón del Valle-Inclán made a name for himself at these *tertulias*, and not only because of his unconventional views on the theatre and literature. He was a dandy and an eccentric with a quirky sense of humour. But his fiery temper sometimes landed him in trouble, one such occasion taking place in 1899 at Madrid's Café de la Montaña, a short-lived rival to the Gijón. Valle-Inclán revelled in controversy and liked nothing more than getting stuck into a rousing debate.

On that day, it had been agreed that a duel would take place between a Portuguese cartoonist living in Madrid named Leal da Câmara and a Spaniard, López del Castillo. Duels were commonplace in Spain, a country obsessed with notions of honour and machismo. The pair had argued heatedly over whether Spanish or Portuguese was the superior nationality, and decided to settle the question with pistols or a little swordplay. It promised to provide lively entertainment at the gathering organised by Valle-Inclán. So he wasn't best pleased when at the last moment the journalist Manuel Bueno Bengoechea hurried into the café and declared that the duel could not legally take place because Leal da Câmara was a minor, not yet 18. Which was true enough.

Valle-Inclán leapt to his feet. 'What do you know about that, you fool?' he bellowed, grabbing a bottle of water and hitting the journalist with it. But Manuel Bueno hit back hard, striking Valle-Inclán on the left wrist with his cane. It caused the cufflink on his shirt to dig into his flesh, an injury Valle-Inclán at first dismissed as a scratch. However, the wound festered and by the time he finally saw a doctor it had infected his entire forearm and turned gangrenous. The only solution was to amputate. It was reported that the writer remained calm throughout the operation, smoking a cigar. When the surgeon afterwards asked how he was feeling he pointed to the absent limb and replied: 'My arm hurts a lot.'

His allies staged a fund-raising event at a theatre and used the proceeds to pay for a prosthetic arm. But Valle-Inclán refused to wear it, citing his dislike for anything artificial. For some time after this debacle, the *tertulias* in Madrid were disputatious affairs, with fiery quarrels between the pro-Valle-Inclán camp and the supporters of Manuel Bueno. In the end, Valle-Inclán, fed up with the divisive situation, approached the journalist in a spirit of reconciliation. 'Let bygones be bygones,' he proclaimed. 'I lost an arm but still have another with which to shake your hand.'

He also tired of having to tell strangers how he had lost his arm, and came up with a new explanation instead: 'One day my servant came to tell me there was nothing in the pantry with which to cook a meal. So I told him: "Cut off this arm and put it in the oven." That's how I lost it.'

Valle-Inclán despised literary realism and as time went on moved closer to the philosophy of anarchism. In his plays *Divine Words* (*Divinas palabras*) and *Bohemian Lights* (*Luces de Bohemia*) he attacked what he regarded as the moralising and sentimentality of bourgeois playwrights. He also satirised the patriotism and militarism of the ruling classes, and their obsequious attitudes towards the monarchy and the Catholic Church. His plays featured mocking portrayals of past Spanish public figures, using obscene language and vulgar imagery; his worst enemy was blandness. He created a tragi-comic theatrical genre he called *esperpento*, meaning grotesque, which anticipated the work of Samuel Beckett, Eugène Ionesco and Jean Genet. As well as being politically subversive, his plays often required staging so complex – including 'supernatural' special effects theatres were unable to supply – that they were classed as 'closet dramas', destined to be read instead of staged.

In reality, the great iconoclast struggled to live up to his bohemian ideals, at times making his living by penning popular serialised novels under a pseudonym. It was ever thus in the world of writers who also have bills to pay and families to support.

A generation of friends

In 1914, Gumersindo García sold the Gran Café de Gijón to an upwardly mobile hairdresser called Benigno López Jabato, with the proviso that it must always remain a café and retain its original name. He needn't have worried. The new owner was keen to preserve its reputation as a prestigious literary establishment, the *tertulias* continued, and the early decades of the twentieth century saw the constant flow through its doors of the period's major cultural figures. For now a new grouping had emerged in Spain, and the Gijón became its base in Madrid. This was the so-called Generation of '27, also known as the Generation of Friends – poets, writers and artists who adopted this appellation following their 1927 act of homage to the

The bearded Ramón del Valle-Inclán with friends and admirers at a tertulia in Madrid's Gran Café Gijón.

Baroque lyric poet Luis de Góngora on the 300th anniversary of his death; they considered him the greatest of Spanish poets, a writer of 'pure' poetry. Federico García Lorca, a leading member of this group, extolled Góngora's ingenious use of metaphor, a fundamental device to the Generation of '27 poets: 'A metaphor unites two opposing worlds thanks to the equestrian jump of the imagination.' Also associated with the group were Lorca's close friends, Salvador Dalí and the filmmaker Luis Buñuel. The three of them had met in the early 1920s while living at Madrid's Residencia de Estudiantes, the student hall of residence, a hothouse of creativity that helped forge their later work. Dalí had rejected the homosexual Lorca's advances, but this had been no bar to their friendship.

Despite being lumped together, the individual members of the Generation of '27 didn't share a sole overriding style or focus beyond their open-minded approach to the arts, their desire to create something wholly new. Sadly, their alliance was brought to an end by the outbreak of the Spanish Civil War in 1936. That was Buñuel's cue to emigrate and he eventually settled in Mexico; Dalí had by then already left for Paris anyway; and soon after the war began the ardent socialist Lorca was tragically killed by General Francisco Franco's military authorities. Other members were imprisoned or forced into exile. A reluctant few remained in Francoist Spain after the Republicans were defeated. The poet Gerardo Diego, unlike most Generation '27 members, supported Franco's nationalists; he stayed and became a prominent figure at the Café Gijón's *tertulias*.

By a twist of fate, the lives of those one-time café combatants of an earlier generation, Ramón del Valle-Inclán and Manuel Bueno Bengoechea, both ended in 1936. Valle-Inclán died aged 69 of bladder cancer, waving away a priest who hoped to give him the last rites, and Bueno was assassinated a few weeks into the Civil War, aged 62. Allegedly suspected of writing for an anti-Republic publication, he was captured and shot by a Republican militia.

War junkie

Among the multi-national writers and journalists covering the war in Spain was, naturally, the adrenalin addict Ernest Hemingway. He had a lifelong love affair with Spain, particularly Madrid, which he called 'the most Spanish of all cities'. Visiting the country many times to write, drink and watch his beloved bullfights, 'Don Ernesto' naturally wouldn't miss the great showdown between Franco's fascist forces and the leftist Republicans. Most bars and cafés in Madrid claim that Hemingway, at one time or another, drank in them, and no doubt he did get tanked-up at many. It's said that at the Café Gijón he once held forth long into the night on bullfights and books. But that's unlikely to have happened while he was covering the Civil War, when he would have been propping up the bar of the Hotel Florida, where the war correspondents congregated. He had a room at the same hotel with his lover, war reporter Martha Gellhorn, later his wife number three.

Apparently, he described the Gijón's intellectual clientele as 'snobby'. But perhaps they were just more interested in getting on with their *tertulia* than in getting drunk with the Americano who liked to stay up all night drinking: 'To go to bed early at night in Madrid marks you as a little queer,' he wrote in his book *The Dangerous Summer*.

> For a long time your friends will feel a little uncomfortable about it. Nobody goes to bed in Madrid until they have killed the night. Appointments with a friend are habitually made for after midnight at the earliest. In no other town that I have ever lived in is there less going to bed for sleeping purposes.

The Spanish Civil War dragged on for three years until, thanks to military support from Hitler, the fascists were victorious in 1939. Atrocities had been committed by both sides and the conflict cost half a million lives. There was widespread destruction, the economy was shattered and millions were starving.

Like bees in a hive

During the war and its immediate aftermath, yet another new company of writers emerged in Spain. Yes, it was time for another generation, this time the Generation of

'36. They were the young novelists, playwrights and poets who had lived through the war and been indelibly marked by the political, social and economic upheavals it created. Their work and careers would be informed by the constraints of living under a military dictatorship, with its censorship of the arts, and decades in which Spanish society was bitterly divided between the war's winners and its losers.

Camilo José Cela, iconoclastic Spanish novelist and controversialist.

The membership criteria for the Generation of '36 were flexible, but it was a convenient label for a collection of literary stylists both during and after the convulsions of the Civil War. Perhaps its most controversial member was Camilo José Cela. His first novel, *La Familia de Pascual Duarte* (*The Family of Pascual Duarte*), was published in 1942, when he was 26. Its characters exist in the margins of society during a period of extreme instability in Spain, their lives full of anguish. The eponymous protagonist is a provincial murderer with no sense of conventional morality, who believes that violence is the only solution to his problems. He relates his life story as he awaits execution in the condemned cell.

It was the first novel to be written in Cela's narrative style, known as *tremendismo* or 'tremendous-ism', which emphasised violence and the grotesque. The book created an uproar and was briefly banned, but became a twentieth-century classic and influenced the future direction of the Spanish novel.

Remarkably, for an experimental writer determined to push against the boundaries of acceptability, the pro-nationalist Cela was himself one of Franco's literary censors in the early 1940s. So he might have predicted that his second novel, *La Colmena* (*The Hive*), written between 1945 and 1950, would fall foul of the country's rigid censorship laws. A depiction of Spain's social and economic traumas in the aftermath of the Civil War through a vast panoply of interwoven characters, the book was banned because of its perceived immorality and eroticism. It was published instead in Buenos Aires, Argentina.

The novel is set in a Madrid café and revolves around the trials and tribulations of its customers. The café Cela used as his model is most often taken to be his regular haunt, the Gijón. The book is composed of short episodic passages, each focusing on a particular character. Altogether, they form a complete picture and conclusion, just as the individual bees in a hive combine to reach a common goal. The novel was intended as a metaphor for the beehive of activity amongst Madrid's desperados, dreamers and deadbeats during the early period of the Franco dictatorship, a time of great poverty and hardship. When the book was finally published in Spain in 1966, it was hailed as a tour de force.

Despite being censored and unable for years to speak about his work in the media, Cela remained loyal to Francoist Spain. During the 1960s, he even worked as an informer for the Spanish secret police by reporting on the activities of dissidents, spying on and betraying other intellectuals who had assumed he was a trusted friend. He suggested to government ministers that dissident writers might be bribed and thus 'converted' by the regime.

The king steps up

During the thirty-six years of Franco's dictatorial rule, his political opponents were supressed with concentration camps, forced labour, imprisonment and execution, leading to 30,000 to 50,000 deaths. But with the death of Franco in 1975, his successor, Prince Juan Carlos of the Bourbon dynasty, became King of Spain and Head of State. Franco had always been distrustful of him, suspecting he had inherited his father's liberal leanings. As it turned out, he was spot on. The new king began the country's transition to a multi-party constitutional democracy with an elected parliament, and within two years, Spain held its first free elections since before the Civil War. Sometimes it takes a monarch to establish a democracy.

There was an amnesty for the officials who had worked under Franco, and Spain never underwent the kind of 'de-Nazification' process that took place in post-war Germany. There was no public naming and shaming of Franco's collaborators, no matter how bloody their hands, as there was of similar people in the former Soviet satellite states after the fall of communism.

And so, the wounds never really healed. There were (and perhaps still are) those who found it hard to forgive Cela for having aligned himself with the Franco dictatorship. One was the Generation of '36 novelist Eusebio García Luengo, who had been on the Republican side during the Civil War. In later life he spent his afternoons chatting and drinking with other writers at the Café Gijón, and eventually appeared to have given up work altogether. One day he was asked by a fellow habitué: 'Eusebio, if you have already given up writing, what do you do now?' Luengo gave a wry smile and replied: 'I am very busy. I dedicate myself twenty-four hours a day to hating Camilo José Cela.'

Cela never paid a price for his political choices, and his stature in the literary world continued to grow. As time went on his work became even more experimental, and in the eyes of some, rather self-indulgent. His book *Cristo versus Arizona*

(*Christ versus Arizona*), for example, tells the story of the legendary gunfight at the O.K. Corral in a single sentence more than a hundred pages long.

Cela had a seemingly infinite capacity for provoking controversy and creating enemies. His *Diccionario secreto* (*Secret Dictionary*), a dictionary of taboo and slang words, scandalised Spanish society, and he was prone to ill-mannered outbursts while giving interviews. Yet as with his Francoist past, none of this damaged his standing on the international stage, and in 1989, he was awarded the Nobel Prize in Literature. Then in 1995 came the Miguel de Cervantes Prize, the lifetime achievement award for writers in the Spanish language. He had previously described receiving it as equivalent to 'being covered with shit'. But when offered it himself, he happily accepted. The following year, Cela even joined the ranks of the Spanish nobility when King Juan Carlos bestowed on him the hereditary title of Marquess of Iria Flavia.

But his provocative acts continued. In 1998, he attended an event commemorating the centenary of the birth of poet García Lorca, but disapproved of the presence of gay groups, claiming he would have preferred a straightforward commemoration without the 'anecdotal' homosexual element. He died four years later, aged 85, after falling out with and disinheriting his son – antagonistic to the end.

A glimpse of glory

Like its Parisian counterparts, the Café de Flore and Café les Deux Magots, the Gran Café Gijón also instituted a literary prize, back in 1949. The aim was in part to promote its *tertulias*. Cela had been one of the prize's founders, and ironically, his implacable foe, Eusebio García Luengo, was its first recipient with his novel *La Primera Actriz* (*The Leading Actress*).

Arguably more books have been written about the Gijón than any other such establishment – twelve in total. They include the 1955 *Chronicle of the Café Gijón* by the journalist and biographer Marino Gómez-Santos, a portrait of 'the last great literary café of Spain'; Francisco Umbral's 1972 autobiography, *The Night I Arrived at Café Gijón*; and the 2007 *Ronda del Gijón*: *An Epoch in the History of Spain* by Marcos Ordóñez, a record of the café from the end of the Civil War to the close of the twentieth century, through the memories, reflections and anecdotes of the writers who frequented it.

Then there is the intriguingly titled 2014 book *Madrid Canalla: Historias Intelectuales y Golfas del Café Gijón* (*Rogue Madrid: Intellectual and Slutty Stories of Café Gijón*) by the poet and bullfighting critic Javier Villán. As he explains:

> To belong to the Gijón tribe you must have been a bohemian when bohemianism still existed, have the police after you or at least the owner of the boarding house where you live and who hasn't been paid. And be more nourished by wine, books and idle time than by good food. To have loved

> to exhaustion and been loved to the limit. And to have participated in love quarrels and bloodless, though wicked, literary brawls. A glimpse of glory is essential, though without too many expectations.

The Gijón has patently been long viewed as a national treasure. Yet these treasures can always be at risk of closure. About a decade ago, the café's licence to use its pavement terrace, on the pedestrianised central reservation of the Paseo de Recoletos boulevard, was up for renewal. Madrid's cash-strapped city council, owner of the land in question, put it out to tender. During the long summer months, three-quarters of the café's revenue comes from its tree-shaded outdoor tables, so to lose this pavement terrace would have tipped the Gijón into bankruptcy.

A commercial entity stepped forward and offered the council twice as much for the use of the terrace area as the café could afford to pay, and for a while, it looked as though greed would win and the Gijón would be shuttered for good. But in the end, following an angry outcry from the literary world, as well as a number of Spanish politicians, both the commercial entity and the council backed down. The café's terrace licence was affordably renewed and the patrons of the venerable Gran Café de Gijón continue to enjoy their al fresco refreshments and socialising unperturbed.

Chapter Fourteen

CAFÉ SLAVIA, PRAGUE

Prague's illustrious Habsburg-era café, the Slavia, is on the ground floor of the imposing building known as the Lažanský Palace. Named after an ancient Slavic goddess, 'the protector of the harvest', whose statue once adorned it, the Slavia occupies the corner of Smetanovo Nábřeží (Smetana Embankment), the thoroughfare which runs alongside the Vltava River, and Národní Avenue, where it faces the National Theatre. The café and the theatre opened in the same year, 1881, and have always enjoyed a close association; from the beginning, the Slavia's regulars included actors and playwrights, stage designers, directors and other theatre workers, as well as theatregoers. It was, after all, the easiest place to pop into before and after performances, or meet with theatrical colleagues.

The café's first style of décor was Viennese Art Nouveau. Later, after the collapse of the Austro-Hungarian Empire and the formation of independent Czechoslovakia, would come the switch to Art Deco. Either way, from its large dual-aspect windows it commanded the best views offered by any Prague coffee house: of the river and its historic Legion Bridge, Prague Castle sitting on its hill across the river, and of the majestic Renaissance Revival architecture of the National Theatre across the road.

It's no coincidence that the embankment here is named after the pioneering composer Bedřich Smetana, regarded as the father of Czech music. His patriotic opera *Libuše*, about the mythical Princess Libuše, sovereign of the Czech tribe and founder of Prague, was composed to mark the inauguration of the National Theatre. Smetana attended this world premiere and received a lengthy standing ovation. The theatre was destroyed in a fire not long afterwards, but it was rebuilt and reopened in November 1883, once again with a performance of *Libuše.* By then Smetana's physical and mental health had deteriorated and he was unable to attend, dying six months later. Sources that claim the Czech composer was a frequenter of the Café Slavia are therefore wide of the mark.

A pint-size cross-dresser

One important figure who undeniably *did* frequent the Slavia, and even immortalised it in his work, was the lyric poet Rainer Maria Rilke. He was born in Prague in 1875 and (like fellow Prague native Franz Kafka) wrote in German. Turn-of-the-century Prague, in the region of Bohemia, was a very divided city. On the one hand, there was the German-speaking population, aligned with the Habsburg monarchy and composed of the wealthier citizens, the bourgeoisie, intellectuals and the Jewish minority. On the other, there were the Czech-speakers, mainly working class and including supporters of the Czech national revival movement. The latter, of course, wanted greater autonomy from the monarchy, and were a rapidly growing population due to the influx of Czechs from the rest of Bohemia (the large western part of today's Czech Republic) and Moravia (its eastern territory).

Each of these two ethnic groups had its own establishments in the city, and the Café Slavia was emphatically in the Czech camp. But the young German-speaker Rilke had good reason to spend time there in the 1890s, soaking up its atmosphere. He was gathering material for two early stories, centring on the tensions between the German-speakers and the Czech nationalists.

Rilke's childhood had been bizarre, to put it mildly. An only child, his father was a railway official and former officer in the Austrian army, and his mother was possessive, controlling and decidedly perverse. When he was born she was still mourning the death of an infant daughter a year earlier, and as if to replace one female child with another, for Rilke's first five years she dressed him in girls' clothing. His father opposed this absurdity but to no effect. 'I had to wear beautiful long dresses,' Rilke recalled many years later, 'and until I started school I went about like a little girl. I think my mother played with me as though I were a big doll.'

Rainer Maria Rilke, *c.*1905.

In a kind of parental tug-of-war, as he grew older his mother interested him in poetry and the French language, whilst his father gave him toy soldiers and imbued in him the concept of military glory. Then, in 1884, when he was 9, his parents' marriage fell apart. At the age of 11 the sensitive and creative child was, no doubt ill-advisedly, sent to a military boarding school in Austria. It wasn't a success and he left five years later due to health problems. The teenager returned to Prague, where he was privately tutored in order to pass the entrance exams for Prague's Charles-Ferdinand University. But he also wrote poems, and his first poetry collection, *Leben und Lieder* (*Life and Songs*), was published when he was 19. A year later, he passed the university entrance exams and commenced his studies in literature, art history and philosophy.

It was during this period that Rilke frequented the Slavia and used it as a setting for his lengthy story, *King Bohush*, inspired by a real-life murder at the time in Prague. The title character of Bohush is a simple-minded hunchback who hobnobs with Czech actors and writers at the café opposite the 'Czech Theatre'. Though in the story it's called the National Café, it is unmistakable as the Slavia. There Bohush gets entangled with a brooding Czech nationalist, a student called Rezek, and his revolutionary cell. Drawn into their underground activities, he shows Rezek a good hiding place for the clandestine group. But when the revolutionaries are discovered and arrested, Rezek mistakenly suspects Bohush of having betrayed them and murders him. Rilke's second story, *The Siblings*, also features the dangerous Rezek, recounting his malign influence on an unsophisticated Czech brother and sister who have moved to the capital from the countryside.

Rilke left Prague at the age of 22 to continue his studies in Munich, where he quickly began a love affair with a much older married woman, the intellectual Lou Andreas-Salomé, who would be his mentor and muse. They did some travelling together, then co-habited for a couple of years in a suburb of Berlin, where Rilke produced his volume containing the two long stories based on Rezek. *Two Stories of Prague* was published in Germany in 1899, when he was 24. But his absorption in the socio-political conflicts between Bohemia's ethnic communities proved fleeting, and Rilke turned his focus on other themes, in particular Christianity and mankind's relationship with God. He never lived in Prague again and grew to dislike the city, dismissing it as a collection of 'subjugated existences'.

Beware the green fairy

At the same time as Rilke abandoned Bohemia, the Art Nouveau painter and illustrator Viktor Oliva returned home to it. He had been living in Paris for a decade, drawn to the artistic community around Montmartre, where he joined a circle of other expat Czech artists and intellectuals. They were Bohemians by both homeland and lifestyle, and it's interesting to find out how the two meanings got lumped together.

In the early nineteenth century, the French began using the term *bohémien* for the Romany peoples of France, whom they wrongly supposed to have reached France in the fifteenth century via Bohemia. As they were wanderers, leading a freewheeling, unconventional lifestyle, the word assumed a broader definition to describe the non-traditional lives of artists, writers, musicians and actors in the cities of Europe. A common theme amongst them was a contempt for money, which meant they were generally poor. This struggling milieu was romanticised in Henri Murger's 1845 collection of autobiographical short stories, *Scènes de la Vie de Bohème* (*Scenes of Bohemian Life*), on which Puccini based his opera *La Bohème*. And where do the penniless free spirits portrayed by Murger – artist, poet, composer, philosopher – hang out as they pursue their dreams? At the Latin Quarter's Café Momus, of course. Their rented room is far too cold, and for lack of fuel, they've been burning their own manuscripts to keep warm …

And so to Viktor Oliva who, following his stint in Paris, returned to his homeland in 1897 to take up a position as picture editor of the popular Czech-language magazine *Zlatá Praha* (*Golden Prague*). He was to do the job for nineteen years, as well as illustrating books by Czech writers and decorating the ceilings of various buildings with his paintings. Having fallen in love with the café life in Paris, it's understandable that he chose to display several of his works in Prague cafés, especially at his favourite, the Slavia, where his most famous work hangs today. This is his 1901 painting, *Piják absintu* (*The Absinthe Drinker*).

***The Absinthe Drinker*, by Viktor Oliva, 1901, which adorns the Café Slavia, Prague.**

While in Paris, Oliva discovered the pleasures and pitfalls of this potent, aniseed-flavoured green spirit. It was strongly associated with bohemian culture, and notable absinthe drinkers have included bohemians such as Lord Byron, Oscar Wilde, Edgar Allen Poe, James Joyce and Paul Verlaine. Absinthe was traditionally known as 'the green fairy' and Oliva's painting depicts a sozzled-looking middle-aged gent sitting at a café table with a glass of the stuff before him. He is alone but for a translucent, naked green female – the fairy in question – perched on the edge of his table. In the background, a waiter looks on dumbfounded; apparently, he too can see the slinky spectre. Ah, *la vie de bohème*.

The Friday Men and the Robots

Oliva died in 1928 at the age of 66 and was buried in an area of Prague's Olšany Cemetery reserved for prominent artists. During the final decade of his life, it would have been virtually impossible for him not to have bumped into Karel Čapek, one of the most important Czech writers of the 1920s and another Café Slavia regular. In 1921, Čapek founded an intellectual circle composed of writers, journalists and politicians called *Pátečníci* (the Friday Men), which met on Friday afternoons, mostly in the garden of his villa in Prague but at times also at the Slavia. They acted as advisors to the politician Tomáš Masaryk, who was instrumental in establishing the independent republic of Czechoslovakia after the First World War, and served as its first president.

Café Slavia, Prague, 1920s.

The robots rebel in Karel Čapek's 1921 play, *Rossum's Universal Robots*.

The Friday Men were strong supporters of the political goals and ideals of Masaryk, a humanist philosopher and firm believer in democratic values. With his American wife and his time living and teaching in London (1915 to 1917), Masaryk's sympathies were with the Anglo-Saxon West and he steered his country firmly in that direction. Whilst denouncing the German 'settlers and colonists' living in Czechoslovakia, he rejected over-zealous Czech chauvinism and fought for a tolerant, if Czech-dominated state.

It was at the Café Slavia that one of the Friday Men, the journalist and political theorist Ferdinand Peroutka, spent much time writing his monumental account of the creation of the Czechoslovak republic and its first constitution: *Budování Statu* (*Building the State*). As well as frequently demanding coffee from the waiters, he would call for documents to be sent to him at the café from President Masaryk's office across the river, at Prague Castle.

In 1925, Karel Čapek started the Czech branch of the international PEN Club (Poets, Essayists, Novelists) and became its president. The organisation's aim was (and is) to promote literature as a means of forging deeper understanding between nations and peoples, which tallied closely with Čapek's own ethos.

By then he had already achieved international success. Though starting his writing career as a journalist alongside his older brother Josef, he made his name as the author of the science fiction play, *R.U.R.* The initials stand for *Rossumovi Univerzální Roboti* (*Rossum's Universal Robots*) and it's a dystopian work about a factory that makes artificial people called *roboti*. It premiered at Prague's National Theatre in 1922. By the following year, it had been translated into thirty languages and was being performed in the UK and around Europe, as well as in America, having introduced the word 'robot' to the English language and the international lexicon of science fiction. It was assumed that Čapek, as the play's author, had invented the word himself, but he explained that his brother Josef had come up with it. Čapek had originally intended to call the factory's creatures *laboři*, from the Latin word for work, *labor*, before deciding it sounded too phony. So Josef suggested *roboti*, which he derived from an archaic Slavic word, *rabota*, denoting the forced labour of serfs.

The play's robots are a metaphor for 'modernity gone mad'. They can think for themselves and are so true to life they are easily mistaken for real people. Initially content to work for humans, they end up rebelling and ultimately bring about the extinction of the human race. It was an astonishingly prescient piece of writing: a century on, we are nervously contemplating this very possibility.

The brothers cut a dash

Josef Čapek started out as his brother's writing collaborator before concentrating on art as a painter of the Cubist school, in addition to working as a book illustrator and cartoonist. He and his brother were very close and lived together for years at

Karel and Josef Čapek. *(Karel Čapek Memorial, Stará Hut, Czech Republic)*

Karel's villa in a quiet residential part of Prague. They were celebrated cultural figures in the newly independent Czechoslovakia, and the dapper pair, sporting colourful scarves and carrying bamboo canes, took frequent constitutionals along the embankment – passing by the Café Slavia and often dropping in. From 1921 onwards, Karel wrote for the influential liberal daily, *Lidové Noviny* (*People's Newspaper*), whilst Josef was the paper's art critic and caricaturist.

The brothers shared a delightful sense of humour. Keen gardeners, they produced a book together, *Zahradníkův rok* (*The Gardener's Year*). Karel wrote the text, full of wry observations on his challenging hobby: 'There are a number of ways of laying out a garden. The best is by taking on a gardener.' Josef meanwhile drew the accompanying comic illustrations. It was published in Prague in 1929 and thanks to the British fondness for gardening, was soon translated into English and published in London too. It's a classic and once again in print.

Another collaboration for Karel Čapek came about as a result of his close friendship with Tomáš Masaryk. His in-depth interviews with the Czech president over a number of years, in which the politician explained his worldview and reflected on his extraordinary life and career – which saw the Czech people move from centuries of Habsburg domination to independent nationhood – were collected together and published in three volumes in the early 1930s as *Talks With T.G. Masaryk*.

Neither man could have imagined that before the decade was over the Czechs would once again have lost their autonomy and been subsumed in an empire – one that by comparison made the Habsburgs seem positively benevolent – and suffer another, equally terrible and much longer foreign subjugation after that. Perhaps it was a blessing that the elderly Masaryk, who had acquired the epithet 'father of his nation', died in 1937, shortly before the darkness descended.

A nation thrown to the wolves

It was alarming enough for the Czechs when the Nazis came to power in Germany. But when Austria was incorporated into the Third Reich with the Anschluss in March 1938, Czechoslovakia was left dangerously exposed on three sides. The Czechs must have suspected that Hitler wouldn't stop there. And their worst fears were realised that September, when the leaders of Great Britain, France and Italy – Neville Chamberlain, Édouard Daladier and Benito Mussolini – trooped off to meet Hitler in Munich and compliantly signed the Munich Agreement. This allowed Hitler to annex Czechoslovakia's Sudetenland regions, populated largely by ethnic Germans.

Karel Čapek died at the age of 48 in December 1938, three months after the break-up of the republic to which he had dedicated so much of his life and work. A heavy smoker who had suffered from ill health all his life, he had caught pneumonia. But according to his friend Ferdinand Peroutka, his spirit had been crushed and he died of a broken heart. Čapek's final article in *Lidové Noviny* was a plea for reconciliation between the countries of Europe. A vain hope.

On 14 March 1939, the Czechoslovak president, Emil Hácha, was summoned to see Hitler in Berlin. As his weak, truncated country was in no position to defend itself, he was easily bullied into signing away its independence. Though Hácha became nominal president of the newly proclaimed German Protectorate of Bohemia and Moravia, the real power lay with the *Reichsprotektor*, Hitler's representative there. The following day, German troops marched into Czechoslovakia.

Like his brother, Josef Čapek had been a staunch democrat and outspoken critic of the Nazis. By the late 1930s, he had received international recognition as an artist, with his works displayed in London and in America. Six months after the Nazis invaded his country he was arrested by the Gestapo and sent to Dachau concentration camp. He was later transferred to Buchenwald, where he spent two and a half years. His artistic talent enabled him to have a somewhat easier time there; he was assigned to a calligraphy workshop and given the task of producing decorative family trees for the camp's SS officers. His next transfer was to the Sachsenhausen concentration camp, where he wrote and illustrated a long poem dedicated to his brother.

Towards the end of the war, Čapek was transported once more and this time it proved a death sentence. He was sent to Bergen-Belsen, then in the midst of a typhus epidemic. For a while, he was well enough to keep writing, and produced a collection of poems. But severely weakened after five and a half years of incarceration in four brutal concentration camps, he fell victim to the disease and died aged 58, a few days before Belsen's liberation by the British Army. His body was never found, but his work was preserved and published after the war as a book, *Poems from a Concentration Camp*.

New times, new tyranny

The long-running ethnic conflict between Bohemia's Germans and Czechs – which once so engrossed Rainer Maria Rilke – was swiftly and ruthlessly brought to an end after the war. All the Sudeten Germans were expelled from Czechoslovakia and their assets expropriated. The newly installed president, Edvard Beneš, who during the war had led the Czech government-in-exile from England, believed in the collective guilt of the Sudeten Germans, who had been such enthusiastic supporters of Hitler. Consequently, thousands of German men, women and children were killed by vengeful Czechs during the post-war expulsion, with the Beneš government indicating it was not particularly averse to such 'popular justice'.

But Beneš's rule was brief. In 1948 he was ousted in the Soviet-sponsored communist coup which saw his nation swallowed up by the USSR, and a broken Beneš died only months later. Courtesy of the occupying Red Army, by that year the communists had also taken over the governments of Poland, Hungary, Romania, Bulgaria and Albania, and with no discernible irony labelled them 'People's Democracies'. A brutal new totalitarianism established itself in the eastern half of Europe – decades of tyranny and suffering by whole populations under Soviet domination. *This* was the ultimate outcome of those countless hours of scheming and conspiring in the cafés of Europe by Lenin, Trotsky and their Bolshevik cohorts in the early years of the twentieth century.

Following Stalin's death in 1953, things began to improve a little in the Eastern Bloc countries, though the Soviet Union still held its satellites in an iron grip; the bloody crushing of the Hungarian Revolution three years later was evidence enough of that. Czechoslovakia was the last country in the bloc to start the process of de-Stalinisation. However, by the mid-1960s, there was a mood of liberalisation in the air, particularly in the creative fields. Writers, artists, performers all hoped to loosen the regime's stranglehold and gain a measure of freedom in their work and lives. Cafés were their natural meeting places, and foremost among them was the Slavia – not only because of its longstanding association with the arts and proximity to the National Theatre, but because it now had fewer rivals. A number of venerable old cafés had been shut down by the communist government for being too bourgeois, their premises converted to other uses.

So it was to the Slavia that young playwrights such as Václav Havel, novelists such as Milan Kundera, and Czech New Wave film-makers Miloš Forman and Ján

Kadár retreated for discussion and debate. One of their number, the poet Jiří Kolář, admitted that he was so poor he usually waited for someone else to pay for his coffee. These dissident intellectuals would grumble, squabble, laugh, gossip and speculate, as they sat at their favourite table by the window. Havel's life in particular revolved around the café. It was there that he met his future wife Olga, and there too that he set up the Circle of Independent Writers to represent the interests of non-communist authors.

One of the Slavia's pre-eminent regulars was the poet Jaroslav Seifert, who later became the first, and only, Czech to receive the Nobel Prize in Literature. 'We used to sit there by the window facing the embankment and drink absinthe,' he reminisced about the café in his memoirs. 'It was a little flirtation with Paris.' He even wrote a poem titled 'Café Slavia', included in his 1967 collection, *Halleyova Kometa* (*Halley's Comet*). In it he imagines the earlier poet Guillaume Apollinaire entering the café through a secret doorway, his head still bandaged from the war, sitting down beside him and reciting his 'brutally beautiful' poems. Seifert honours the poet by drinking absinthe – which is 'greener than everything that is green' – and when he looks out of the window at the river, it's not the Vltava that he sees but the Seine. Apollinaire had briefly visited Prague in 1902 and mentioned the city in his seminal stream-of-consciousness poem, 'Zone'. For Seifert, that fleeting connection was inspiration enough.

He'd been an ardent communist in his youth before growing disenchanted with communism, and had worked primarily as a journalist. But after the post-war communist takeover he was blacklisted and forbidden to practise journalism. So it was poetry he turned to, ultimately receiving state recognition and being awarded important prizes. In 1967, he was given the rare honour of being named *národní umělec*, 'national artist'. But he'd long hoped for an end to the state control of literature, and must have felt his dreams had at last been realised with the advent of the Prague Spring.

The tanks roll in

In January 1968, the reformist Alexander Dubček was elected First Secretary of the Communist Party of Czechoslovakia. Intent on democratising the regime, he ushered in a range of new rights and freedoms for the people of his country. Unsurprisingly, this didn't go down well with the country's Soviet overlords. Eight months later, on 21 August, they did the usual: they sent in the tanks and Warsaw Pact troops to suppress the Prague Spring reforms.

Civilian resistance continued for months but it was low level and largely peaceful. The only reason the invasion was not a repetition of the Soviets' carnage in Hungary during the 1956 Uprising, was that the Czechs did not engage in armed resistance. The Czech military stood back, no one blew up Russian tanks with Molotov cocktails, and there was no do-or-die revolution. Nonetheless, some did find a world-shocking method of protest against the crushing of Dubček's reforms. In January 1969, 20-year-old university student Jan Palach set himself on fire in Prague, dying of his burns three days later. His funeral turned into a mass demonstration against the Soviet invasion and inspired two other Czechs – Jan Zajic and Evžen Plocek – to commit suicide by self-immolation in the subsequent months, followed by similar acts of protest elsewhere in the Soviet bloc.

Dubček was removed from office in April 1969 and expelled from the Communist Party, which was duly purged of all other liberal-minded members. The new First Secretary (and later President), Gustáv Husák, reversed virtually all the reforms and introduced the period referred to, depressingly, as 'normalisation'. Jaroslav Seifert, an outspoken Dubček supporter, had been president of the Czech Writers' Union but was now stripped of the position and officially declared persona non grata. From then on, he was able to disseminate his work only in samizdat form, or else through émigré Czech publishers in the West.

Husák proceeded to remove liberals from the professions, from academia and the arts, forcing them to take up manual jobs. Václav Havel had spoken out in support of Dubček and his reforms in the early days of the Soviet invasion. Now banned from working in the theatre, he took up a job at a brewery. But of course he made good use of this unexpected experience by creating plays out of it. They received wide distribution in samizdat form and further cemented his reputation as a leading anti-communist writer, the precise opposite of what Husák had wanted.

Spies in the Slavia

All this *normalisation*, i.e. clampdown on freedom, spelled trouble for the clientele of the Café Slavia. As in so many earlier periods of history, in so many other places, the authorities regarded gatherings at coffee houses with the utmost suspicion. As haunts of the intelligentsia, they were also hotbeds of subversion and dissent. The Czech secret police, amongst the most repressive in the Soviet satellite states, hit upon the clever idea of recruiting café waiters as their informers. It wouldn't be difficult for them to overhear snippets of conversations, the dangerous words of agitators.

It's impossible to know how many 'enemies of the state' were collared in this way by the secret police. But their earwigging at the Slavia didn't deter dissidents such as Havel; it remained his chosen retreat. Could he have imagined, as he stirred his coffee and gazed out of the window at the distant Prague Castle, seat of the President of the Republic of Czechoslovakia, that one day he would be sitting there in Husák's place?

In 1977, Havel helped initiate the Charter 77 manifesto, in reaction to the imprisonment the previous year of the Czech psychedelic rock band, The Plastic People of the Universe. As well as sporting hair that was unacceptably long for communist tastes, the band were part of a greater underground cultural movement in Prague and the regime was determined to make an example of them. All around the city young male fans of the Plastics started growing their hair long in solidarity.

Charter 77 criticised the Czech government for failing to implement the human rights provisions in several documents to which it had been a signatory. Seifert was one of the first to sign the manifesto and in the end almost 2,000 more had joined him – writers, politicians, playwrights, actors, journalists – many of their signatures collected at the Café Slavia. The government's crackdown against them was swift and harsh. They were fired from their jobs, their children barred from educational opportunities, and there were trials and prison sentences. Some were forced to collaborate with the secret police.

Havel endured several spells in prison for his political activities, the longest being his four-year sentence from 1979 to 1983. Each time, after his release, he would make his way to the Slavia to re-join his friends: 'I was important for a while, regaling the others with stories of what I went through,' he wrote.

But at the end of that decade – in the wake of Russian President Gorbachev's *glasnost* and *perestroika* reforms – he launched his Civic Forum movement, uniting the different dissident groups in Czechoslovakia with the aim of finally overthrowing the communist government. It was phenomenally successful. After only ten days of mass demonstrations, the four-decade-long totalitarian regime collapsed, in November 1989, like the proverbial house of cards. It was all so smooth they named it the Velvet Revolution. Havel was elected president a month later and installed a genuine democracy. The false, Soviet-style 'people's democracies' of Eastern Europe were all swiftly consigned to history's scrapyard.

Victory over stupidity

The new Czech president's involvement with the Café Slavia was far from over. The establishment had a bumpy few years in the 1990s. The premises were leased by an American company, which closed down the café in 1992, and due to a legal dispute over ownership it remained shut, its fate uncertain. Having lost none of his crusading zeal (or sense of humour) Václav Havel started a petition against the closure, declaring:

> We strongly protest against the fact that for three years now the Slavia Café, this important and traditional meeting place of Prague intellectuals, students and the elderly, has been closed to the public without any justification or defence. We call on the company that leases this café to open it to the public without delay. Failure to do so will seriously damage the good relations of the Prague intelligentsia with capitalism and with the United States.

The twenty-first-century Café Slavia, Prague.

Václav Havel, lifelong habitué of the Café Slavia.

He joined a crowded sit-in demonstration to hammer home the point.

It worked. The American speculators were banished and the building taken over by the Academy of Performing Arts. After restoring it to its former Art Deco splendour, the Slavia reopened in 1997. Havel called it 'a victory over stupidity'.

And so it was to this august and much-loved institution that he repaired, tired but elated, at the end of an evening at the National Theatre in February 2003. He'd received a standing ovation there, having just left office after serving two terms and thirteen years as president.

In November 2021, ten years after Václav Havel's death, a bronze bust of him by sculptor Marie Šeborová was unveiled at the Café Slavia, and given pride of place by the window.

Chapter Fifteen

COFFEE HOUSES OF THE AMERICAN REVOLUTION

Spain, Portugal, Holland, Belgium, Italy, France, Great Britain. All were colonial powers which at some point relinquished – willingly or not – their colonies. But in only one case did the coffee house play an active role in a European power's loss of overseas territories, and that was the British Empire and its rebellious colonies in America.

The Boston Tea Party, one of history's most memorable protests, took place on the night of 16 December 1773. The American colonists, British subjects all, were heavily taxed by the British government, despite having no representation in Parliament. They considered this unconstitutional, a clear violation of their rights as Englishmen. *No taxation without representation!* they cried and went on crying.

Earlier that year, Parliament had passed the Tea Act, requiring the colonists to purchase only British tea imported by the struggling East India Company, on which they had to pay import duty, unlike tea shipped in from elsewhere. This was one injustice too far. So on that cold December night a large group of protesters belonging to the Sons of Liberty – a clandestine political organisation founded to advance colonists' rights in the Thirteen American Colonies – took matters into their own hands in an imaginative way. Disguised as Mohawk warriors, they slipped aboard three British ships in Boston Harbor and dumped their cargos of tea (45 tons in all) into the water. To the British government this was an act of treason. They closed Boston Harbor to trade and punished the colony of Massachusetts Bay by passing more oppressive acts, bound to result in even stronger colonial resistance. And so the countdown to revolution began.

After the sinking of those 342 chests of tea, tea drinking fell out of fashion in the American colonies, being seen as too British, and coffee became the drink of choice for American patriots. As in Europe, public coffee houses served as important meeting points for political activists and rebellious types, who gathered in them to conspire over their coffee cups. It was with sound reason that conservatives back home in England derided American coffee houses as 'seminaries of sedition' (not unlike the London coffee houses of a century earlier).

A fire-breathing dragon

In New England the history of coffee is closely interwoven with the story of its inns and taverns, where it was served alongside alcoholic beverages, so they were often called 'coffee taverns'. Boston's most important de facto coffee house at that time was the Green Dragon Tavern, established on Union Street (then Green Dragon Lane) in Boston's North End in 1697. Mounted above the front door of the three-storey brick building was a copper dragon, which, as copper always does due to oxidation, had long turned green. The tavern would one day be described by the prominent nineteenth-century American lawyer and statesman Daniel Webster as the 'Headquarters of the Revolution'.

Boston was New England's social centre, and the Green Dragon the heart of Boston's social and business life, where all manner of patrons got together, from colonial governors and officials of the British Crown, to anti-British conspirators and future Founding Fathers of America. The Sons of Liberty (dubbed the Liberty Boys) held covert meetings in its basement; it was where they had planned the Boston Tea Party. Silversmith and arch patriot Paul Revere, key member of the Sons of Liberty, lived nearby and it had long been his haunt. The Green Dragon was home to St Andrew's Lodge of the Freemasons – Revere was a stalwart member – which had purchased the tavern in order to hold its meetings in an upstairs room. Before long, Revere had become the Lodge's Master.

Also based at the Green Dragon was the Boston Caucus, an informal but influential organisation linked to Samuel Adams, the political philosopher and

The Green Dragon coffee tavern in Boston, 1773.

later Founding Father. The Caucus were avid conspirators, involved in the Boston Tea Party. The Boston Committee of Correspondence also held their meetings there: each of the Thirteen Colonies had such a committee (another idea of Samuel Adams), together forming an underground network through which opposition to the British Parliament could be coordinated by writing secret letters. The committees were instrumental in establishing the First Continental Congress, which met in Philadelphia in the autumn of 1774.

In the spring of the following year, Paul Revere and his revolutionary circle were busy observing the activities of British soldiers stationed in the Massachusetts Bay area, and convening in the Green Dragon basement to share the intelligence they had gleaned. After learning of plans for the British Army's invasion of the towns of Lexington and Concord, it was from the Green Dragon that Revere set off on his famous 'midnight ride' of 18 April 1775, to warn the Yankees that the British were coming. The first military engagements of the American War of Independence took place the following day.

Stamping out injustice

Meanwhile in Philadelphia, William Penn's 'city of brotherly love', the most revolutionary coffee house was the Old London, opened on the corner of Front Street and Market Street in 1754 by printer, bookseller and publisher William Bradford. A true American patriot, he published *The Pennsylvania Journal*, each issue carrying the image of a snake chopped into segments with the motto 'Unite or Die', a reference to the separate American colonies (variations of the symbol were also used by Paul Revere and Benjamin Franklin).

The Old London Coffee House quickly became the place to talk politics and conduct business. It was a familiar landmark, centrally located in the business district and adjacent to the waterfront, an ideal rendezvous spot for merchants and storekeepers expressing their discontent with the slew of unwelcome new legislation from the British Parliament.

Given the nature of his own businesses, it wasn't surprising that Bradford had been a particularly vocal opponent of the Stamp Act of 1765, which required printed materials in the colonies to be produced on paper from London containing an embossed revenue stamp, proving that the tax on it had been paid. The materials affected included legal documents, magazines, newspapers and many other paper products used throughout the colonies. What's more, the tax had to be paid in British, not colonial, currency. Bradford attacked Benjamin Franklin for acquiescing to it; when Franklin realised the extent of the colonists' anger, he changed his mind.

When several Philadelphia merchants and store owners assembled at the Old London Coffee House to discuss their response to the new Stamp Act, their discourse quickly escalated into personal threats against Philadelphia's tax collector, John Hughes. The poor official was so terrified he later recalled being forced to protect

THE OLD LONDON COFFEE HOUSE, PHILADELPHIA.

The corner house in Philadelphia, formerly home to the Old London Coffee House.

himself with firearms in case he had to 'stand a siege', while his friends patrolled the neighbourhood 'between my house and the Coffee House'. On another occasion, on the street in front of the Old London, a newspaper published in Barbados and bearing the hated revenue stamp was publicly set alight, to the cheers of bystanders.

In 1774, Bradford was named as the official printer for the First Continental Congress, and in that role printed the formal resolutions, broadsides and documents issued by the Congress – most famously the Declaration of Rights. During those years just before the revolution local leaders in Philadelphia used its coffee houses to stage the ritual destruction of hated statutes and decrees, as well as to sign and circulate their own political documents. The Old London and its competitor establishments truly were at the red-hot core of political activity in those heady days. As the Massachusetts politician John Adams (destined to be the second President of the United States) observed: 'The deliberations of Congress are impenetrable secrets, but the conversations of the city and the coffee house are free and open.'

Bradford was already middle-aged when the revolution broke out, but resolved to fight nevertheless. He left his business in the hands of his son, Thomas, and joined the Pennsylvania militia. A major at first, he was later promoted to colonel.

The British captured Philadelphia in September 1777. As the seat of the Continental Congress, it had been in the sights of British General William Howe, who knew its capture would have marked a decisive victory. But the Congress deprived Howe of this prize by moving its operations to a more secure location a week earlier. After almost nine months of occupation, during which the British officer corps enjoyed the luxuries and comforts of Philadelphia's finest homes (and coffee houses), the Redcoats departed the city of brotherly love.

William Bradford meanwhile saw action in several battles. In New Jersey he was wounded in the Battle of Princeton; persistently plagued by his injury, he resigned from the militia and returned to Philadelphia following the British withdrawal.

Teatime in New York

In Manhattan, the Merchants Coffee House had gained a reputation as a gathering-place for patriots eager to break free from the rule of King George III. Opened in 1737 on the corner of Water Street and Wall Street (which in those days led straight to the waterfront and the East River wharves), it was a typical New England venue: the ground floor contained the coffee house, whilst the first floor had a long public assembly room. One feature distinguishing eighteenth-century American coffee houses from their European counterparts was that they doubled as civic forums, places where council meetings and other public events were held, even court trials. (Another difference was that, unlike in England and France, they weren't breeding grounds for literary innovation – chiefly because there was a dearth of professional writers living in the colonies at that time.)

As it was located near the Meal Market, where grains were sold and merchants congregated for trading purposes, the Merchants Coffee House was a hub for the business community. In addition to the purely commercial organisations that gathered in its long room, other bodies regularly met there in their early days: the Society of Arts, Agriculture and Economy; New York Marine Society; Freemasons; Whig Society; Society of the New York Hospital; Society of the Sons of St. Patrick; Society for Promoting the Manumission of Slaves; Society for the Relief of Distressed Debtors, etc. But in the 1770s, as the conflict between the Thirteen Colonies and the British government reached its zenith, the upstairs assembly room most often saw heated public debates on the pressing political issues of the day. Its proprietor at the time was a widow and estimable businesswoman, Mrs Mary Ferrari.

In April 1774, the tea ship *Nancy*, after being turned away from Boston, sought to land its cargo in New York. Commanded by a wary Captain Lockyer, it had landed to the south of New York City at Sandy Hook, with a cargo of 698 cases of tea from the East India Company (double the number destroyed in Boston). Alerted by the Sons of Liberty, local patriots took control of the ship. Lockyer was escorted into the city and taken to the Merchants Coffee House, where he was confronted by the Liberty Boys, who demanded that he sail back to England, together with the tea, or lose his life. He agreed readily enough and began to make the necessary arrangements; meanwhile the coffee house became his quarters.

A few days later, another British ship, the *London*, arrived under the command of Captain Chambers. Though Chambers protested that he had no tea aboard, the Liberty Boys had already received word from Philadelphia that there were eighteen chests of the stuff hidden on the ship. An angry mob boarded the *London* – this time no one bothering to disguise himself as a native Indian warrior – Chambers was seized and the ship searched. When the tea was discovered, the hated symbol of unfair taxation was chucked into the harbour; the patriots of Manhattan knew how to throw a tea party too. The empty tea chests were then carried into the city, where they were used to ignite bonfires in the streets. Chambers was threatened with his life but managed to escape, and a few days later, the *Nancy* sailed for England with the two chastened captains, Lockyer and Chambers, aboard.

The Crown was predictably furious, especially as New York had been deemed a Loyalist stronghold. In May 1774, a general assembly of citizens was held at the Merchants Coffee House to discuss how best to liaise with the Massachusetts colony and coordinate their efforts in resisting British oppression. A year later, in the immediate aftermath of the battles at Lexington and Concord, mass meetings of New York citizens took place at the coffee house and led to the formation of the Committee of One Hundred. This group of worthies would convene at the coffee house's upstairs assembly room to administer public affairs until New York's revolutionary provisional government, the Provincial Congress, was created. And so the Merchants Coffee House was in effect, briefly, the seat of the colony's government.

The members of the Committee of One Hundred were still essentially loyal to the Crown but opposed to its parliament, which, being denied representation in it, they considered unconstitutional. Writing to the acting governor of New York, Cadwallader Colden, they informed him that whilst they had taken up arms, 'it is not with design to oppose, but to strengthen government in the due exercise of constitutional authority'. Nevertheless, all loyalists within their jurisdiction were disarmed, and there was much tarring and feathering by irate mobs of anyone standing in the way of independence: tax collectors, customs officials and avowed supporters of George III. The committee was officially replaced by the New York Provincial Congress on 23 May 1775.

Washington slips away … then returns in triumph

After America's Continental Army, commanded by George Washington, out-manoeuvred and outgunned the British in the eleven-month siege of Boston in March 1776, Washington relocated his troops to New York to defend the vital port at the southern end of Manhattan Island. Realising the harbour would provide a strategically important base for the Royal Navy, he established defences there and waited for the British to attack. Meanwhile, the Merchants Coffee House served as a welcome retreat for his officers.

In early June, Washington learned that the British fleet had set sail from their temporary refuge at Halifax, Nova Scotia, and was heading towards New York. By the end of the month the fleet had appeared: within hours, forty-five British ships dropped anchor in Lower New York Bay. The population of New York went into a panic at the sight of them and the soldiers of the Continental Army hastened to their posts.

On 6 July, news reached New York that, just two days earlier, the Continental Congress, representative body for the Thirteen Colonies, had voted for independence from Great Britain. Washington ordered several brigades to march on to the city's commons to hear a reading of the Declaration of Independence. Afterwards an excited crowd ran down to Bowling Green with ropes and bars and tore down the equestrian statue of George III.

But the jubilation didn't last long. In late August, New Yorkers heard the cannon blasts which heralded the Battle of Long Island (also known as the Battle of Brooklyn), from across the East River. It would see the Yankee army roundly defeated by British forces, who then invaded New York and gained access to its vital port. Luckily, Washington and his troops were able to make a daring nighttime escape, retreating across New Jersey and into Pennsylvania. Stunned to find that the commander-in-chief had slipped through their hands, the British declared martial law in New York and held the city for seven long years until the end of the war.

The Merchants Coffee House made the best of the British occupation. As before, it was the centre of trading; the Chamber of Commerce resumed its sessions in the long room, and it became a marketplace for the buying and selling of ships. It acquired a new landlord, John Stachan, who evidently hoped to remain in favour with the occupiers. In a public announcement, he promised his customers 'constant and best attendance. Breakfast from seven to eleven, soups and relishes from eleven to half past one. Tea, coffee, etc. in the afternoon, as in England.'

With assistance from the French, the Continental Army forced the British to surrender at Yorktown, Virginia, in 1781, and the Americans effectively won their war. Fighting didn't formally finish, though, for another two years. In September 1783, Great Britain recognised the independence of the United States in the Treaty of Paris and, two months later, the British Army withdrew from New York. In its wake, General Washington arrived from his headquarters north of the city. Mounted on his white charger, he triumphantly led the Continental Army across the Harlem River, through the centre of Manhattan, on to Broadway and down to the Battery at the island's southern tip, with much cheering and waving of the Stars and Stripes along the way.

Last hurrah

There was one last significant decade ahead for the Merchants Coffee House. In 1784, a group of citizens met there to form the city's first financial institution, the Bank of New York. The leader of this group was no less than Alexander Hamilton,

Merchants Coffee House on a corner of Wall Street, New York.

the revolutionary colonel, brilliant statesman and Founding Father, who was still only 27 years old. An expert in economics and banking, he would go on to be the first Secretary of the Treasury during George Washington's presidency – and centuries later, the star of an eponymous hit musical. The coffee house on the corner of Wall Street was also the site of the first public sale of stocks by sworn brokers, marking the birth of the New York Stock Exchange, still on the same street.

But the finest moment of glory for the Merchants Coffee House came on 23 April 1789, when Washington, the recently elected first President of the United States, attended a reception there in his honour. He was greeted at the entrance by the governor of the state, the mayor of the city, and a host of local dignitaries. A week later, he stood on the balcony of Federal Hall, a little further up Wall Street, to take his oath of office as President.

Having earned its place in the history of the United States, the coffee house was finally destroyed by fire in 1804.

Gone but not forgotten

Though William Bradford's publishing enterprise continued to thrive after his return to Philadelphia from his military service, the fortunes of his coffee house did not and he gave it up in 1780. The premises then fell into the hands of one John Pemberton, who put such strict conditions on the person running it ('no cursing, swearing … and under a penalty of £100 he will not allow or suffer any person to use, or play at, or divert themselves with cards, dice, backgammon, or any other unlawful game') that naturally, the place closed a few years later. Those 'ungodly' activities were, after all, quite well tolerated at other coffee houses of the day, and in part, why they were so popular.

Towards the end of the eighteenth century, the Old London was bought by James Stokes, who converted it into his home and a store. In the following decades, it housed a variety of businesses, such as the tobacconist and clothing store depicted in an illustration from *circa* 1854. Three decades later, by then dilapidated and abandoned, the old building once a crucible of home-grown revolutionary fervour was finally torn down.

As for Boston's celebrated Green Dragon, it was thoughtlessly demolished in 1832 to be replaced by a humdrum warehouse. But that cradle of rebellion wasn't forgotten; a commemorative plaque later appeared to remind the public that:

> On this spot stood
> The Green Dragon Tavern
> The secret meet place of the
> Sons of Liberty,
> And in the words of Webster, the
> Headquarters of the Revolution.
> To mark a site forever as
> Memorable as the birthplace of American freedom,
> this tablet is placed by the
> Massachusetts Society of the Sons of Revolution.

Appendix One

Coffee's Greatest Champion, Honoré de Balzac

It would be a gross understatement to say that the legendary French novelist loved his coffee. In fact he was totally addicted to it.

More often than not, Balzac drank his coffee not in a café but at home, prepared by his own hands, following a meticulous routine. He used three kinds of coffee beans – Bourbon, Martinique and Mocha – purchased at three different shops in Paris, and then finely ground. He brewed up the thick aromatic elixir in a large *cafetière*, which would keep his coffee warm for hours.

Balzac's habit was to put on his comfy dressing gown and write concentratedly throughout the night, from midnight to at least noon the following day, during which he reputedly consumed up to fifty cups of coffee. His literary output was accordingly prodigious: more than a hundred novels, plays and short story collections.

His friends observed that he became bad-tempered and cynical when deprived of coffee for long. Ultimately, this super-caffeinated lifestyle proved destructive to his constitution, and he died of heart failure aged 51 … but not before leaving for posterity his cogent thoughts and theories on his beverage of choice.

From Balzac's *Treatise on Modern Stimulants* (which also covers tea, alcohol, tobacco and sugar):

> I have observed [coffee's] effects on an epic scale. Coffee roasts your insides. Many people claim coffee inspires them, but as everybody knows, coffee only makes boring people even more boring. Think about it: though more grocers in Paris are staying open until midnight, few writers are actually getting

Honoré de Balzac.

> wittier. But … coffee sets the blood in motion and stimulates the muscles; it accelerates the digestive processes, chases away sleep, and gives us the capacity to engage a little longer in the exercise of our intellects … Coffee affects the diaphragm and the nerves of the stomach, from which it reaches the brain by barely perceptible radiations which escape complete analysis; that aside, we may surmise that our flow of nerves conducts an electricity emitted by coffee when we drink it.
>
> Coffee's power changes over time. Rossini has personally experienced some of these effects, as, of course, have I. 'Coffee,' Rossini told me, 'is an affair of fifteen or twenty days; just the right amount of time, fortunately, to write an opera.' This is true. But the length of time during which one can enjoy the benefits of coffee can be extended … All of you leading lights, who burn the midnight oil, come close and listen to the gospel of alertness and intellectual effort!

He continues:

> The coffee falls into your stomach and straightaway there is a commotion. Ideas begin to move like the battalions of the *Grande Armée* on the battlefield, and the battle begins. Memories arrive at full gallop, flags flying. The light cavalry of comparisons deliver a magnificent charge, the artillery of logic rushes in with its wagons and ammunition, the shafts of wit appear like sharpshooters. Characters rise up, the paper covers itself with ink – for the nightly labour begins and ends with torrents of this black water, just as a battle opens and concludes with black gunpowder … An observation: among certain weak natures, coffee produces only a kind of harmless mental congestion; instead of feeling animated, these people feel drowsy and they say that coffee makes them sleep. Such individuals … are poorly equipped for intellectual undertakings.

Balzac liked to grind his coffee, but not to mince his words.

Appendix Two

In Extremis: the Final Haven

During the Second World War, the Jews of Nazi-occupied Warsaw were forced to live under unimaginably desperate circumstances. Europe's largest Jewish community, numbering some 400,000, they were driven into a ghetto of only 1.3 square miles. The food rations allowed them by the German authorities were woefully inadequate and the overcrowded, unsanitary conditions soon brought a typhus epidemic. The most vulnerable – the elderly, the infirm and the very young – began to perish.

Political, cultural and educational institutions were banned. Synagogues, cinemas and libraries were closed. But for those with wealth, there was a last remaining refuge and source of hope: the café. Out on the streets there was confusion, despair and death, a living hell. But in a café, almost as if it were a separate planet existing in its own orbit, people clung to an air of normality.

Most of these establishments were to be found on Leszno Street. Even before the ghetto was sealed off by a 10-foot wall in November 1940, several cafés offering a wide range of live musical entertainments had been opened on this busy thoroughfare. It was jokingly referred to as 'the Broadway of the Warsaw Ghetto'. Here was an ample supply of black market coffee, alcohol and food almost like the pre-war days.

The largest and most handsomely furnished was the Café L'Ourse. Its customers' mandatory Star of David armband was the only indication that they were victims of persecution. Their faces were neither despairing nor emaciated; they could afford to eat and drink. This small, select group of ghetto inhabitants could enjoy the comforts, the music of the orchestra, the dancing and the company of their friends and associates, because they possessed the one thing capable of prolonging life: money.

The ghetto's intellectual elite congregated at the Café Sztuka (Art Café). It staged cabaret shows, topical political sketches, readings by well-known literary figures such as the poet and lyricist Władysław Szlengel. Music was provided by (amongst others) Władysław Szpilman, the subject of the 2002 Roman Polanski film *The Pianist*; the glamorous pre-war singing star Wiera Gran, whom Szpilman often accompanied on the piano; and the young soprano Marysia Ajzensztadt, dubbed 'the Nightingale of the Ghetto'. The celebrated musician and composer Artur Gold, meanwhile, performed with a jazz band at the Café Splendid.

The Warsaw Ghetto's Café Sztuka, photographed by a German Army photographer for propaganda purposes in May 1941.

Marysia Ajzensztadt singing at the Café Sztuka.

But these cafés supplied something else besides nourishment for the body and soul: they were a conduit for continued existence. It was where speculators and black marketeers huddled around tables with their clients, quietly sealing deals, because as always there were profits to be made. And it was where smugglers arranged their dangerous missions. At least 80 per cent of food in the ghetto came from smuggling, much of it carried out by children as young as 6, who were small enough to slip through concealed gaps in the ghetto wall. Without this risky clandestine activity, everyone would have soon starved to death. But thieves and collaborators were also known to hang around in the cafés: you had to be on your guard.

It was to the cafés, too, where chancers went hoping to make contact with a canny fixer, someone who knew how to bribe a Nazi guard and perhaps help a Jew escape beyond the wall to the 'Aryan' part of Warsaw. A few, including Wiera Gran, succeeded. Of course, the vast majority did not. From the summer of 1942, the Jews were systematically deported and killed. Less than a year later, following the heroic last-ditch Warsaw Ghetto Uprising, the remaining inhabitants were finished off. Then the Wehrmacht razed the entire area.

The ghetto's café scene was a brief, fiercely burning light in the darkness – an expression of anti-Nazi dissent. For a community about to disappear, it kept hope alive a little longer and offered a last chance to experience some of life's diversions. It had its shady aspects and its critics, but was admirable for all that.

Contact Information

Queen's Lane Coffee House
40 High Street, Oxford OX1 4AP
Tel. +44 1865 240082
https://www.qlcoffeehouse.com

Café Procope
13 rue de l'Ancienne Comédie, Paris 75006
Tel. +33 1 40 46 79 00
https://www.procope.com

Caffè Florian
57 Piazza San Marco, Venice 30124
Tel. +39 041 520 56 41
https://caffeflorian.com

Antico Caffè Greco
86 Via dei Condotti, Rome 00187
Tel. +39 06 679 1700
https://anticocaffegreco.eu

Café Central
14 Herrengasse, Vienna 1010
Tel. +43 (1) 533 37 63-61
https://cafecentral.wien/en

Café Sperl
11 Gumpendorfer Strasse, Vienna 1060
Tel. +43 1 5864158
https://www.cafesperl.at

New York Café
9–11 Erzsébet körút, Budapest 1073
Tel. +36 1 886 6167
https://newyorkcafe.hu

Café de Flore
172 Boulevard Saint-Germain, Paris 75006
Tel. +33 1 45 48 55 26
https://cafedeflore.fr

Café Odeon
2 Limmatquai, Zürich 8001
Tel. +41 44 251 16 50
https://odeon.ch/en

Café Luitpold
11 Briennerstrasse, Munich 80333
Tel. +49 89 2428750
https://www.cafe-luitpold.de

Gran Café de Gijón
21 Paseo Recoletos, Madrid 28004
Tel. +34 915 21 54 25
http://cafegijon.com

Café Slavia
1012/2 Smetanovo nábřeží, Prague 1
Tel. +420 224 218 493
https://www.cafeslavia.cz

Acknowledgements

With the changes of ownership, wars, fires, financial misfortunes and societal vagaries that inevitably beset businesses that have been in operation over centuries, it is unsurprising that the cafés featured in this book have been generally unable to maintain an archive of materials chronicling their history. There are a couple of exceptions: the Florian and the Luitpold have modest collections of illustrations and other materials, and have helpfully allowed me the use of them. But for the rest I've made use of the excellent digital archives available online, with their wealth of material now in the public domain.

The American digital library, the Internet Archive, with its 37.5 million books and 4.6 million images, is a wonderful boon for any writer's research. The digitised library of books freely available on the Project Gutenberg website is also an invaluable depository. Wikimedia Commons is a hugely useful source of images in the public domain, as is the online artworks encyclopaedia, WikiArt. We are fortunate to have them all.

A special thanks to my friend Robin Ashenden, talented writer and editor, for reading my manuscript and giving me the benefit of his advice, and to the friends who accompanied me on my little jaunts around Europe to visit cafés featured in this book. Thanks also to my brother Val, a long-time resident of Munich and inveterate history buff, for his assistance with the Luitpold chapter.

Sources

Books

Bakewell, Sarah, *At the Existentialist Café: Freedom, Being & Apricot Cocktails* (Vintage, London, 2017)

Biderman, Bob, *A People's History of Coffee and Cafés* (Black Apollo Press, Cambridge, 2013)

Brody, Paul, *The Real Midnight in Paris: A History of the Expatriate Writers in Paris That Made Up the Lost Generation* (Golgotha Press Inc., Anaheim, California, 2012)

Brook, Stephen, *The Double Eagle: Vienna, Budapest, Prague* (Hamish Hamilton, London, 1988)

Carl, Klaus H. and Charles, Victoria, *The Viennese Secession* (Parkstone Press International, New York, 2020)

Deming, Brian and Hiff, Ted, *Hitler and Munich: A historical guide to the sights and addresses of Munich important to Adolf Hitler, his followers and his victims* (Verlag Anton Plenk KG, Berchtesgaden, 1988)

Ellis, Markman, *The Coffee-House: A Cultural History* (Weidenfeld & Nicolson, London, 2004)

Fitch, Noel Riley, *The Grand Literary Cafés of Europe* (New Holland Publishers Ltd, London, 2006)

Hamann, Brigitte, *Hitler's Vienna: A Dictator's Apprenticeship* (Oxford University Press, Oxford, 1999)

Hemingway, Ernest, *A Moveable Feast* (Charles Scribner's Sons, New York, 1964)

Herzl, Theodor, *Old New Land* (Markus Wiener Publishing and the Herzl Press, New York, 1987)

Hofmann, Paul, *The Viennese: Splendour, Twilight, and Exile* (Anchor Press, New York, 1988)

Huemer, Christina, *Spellbound By Rome: Anglo-American Community in Rome, 1890–1914* (Palombi Editori, Rome, 2013)

Judt, Tony, *Past Imperfect: French Intellectuals, 1944–1956* (New York University Press, New York and London, 2011)

Kopleck, Maik, *Past Finder: Munich 1933–1945* (Christoph Links Verlag, Berlin, 2007)

Large, David Clay, *Where Ghosts Walked: Munich's Road to the Third Reich* (W.W. Norton & Co., New York, 1997)

Lukacs, John, *Budapest 1900: A Historical Portrait of a City and its Culture* (Weidenfeld & Nicholson, New York, 1988)

Mann, Klaus, *The Turning Point* (Markus Wiener Publishers, Princeton, 1995)

Meredith, Don, *Where the Tigers Were: Travels Through Literary Landscapes* (University of South Carolina Press, Columbia, South Carolina, 2001)

Mesterházi, Lajos, *Budapest Anno* (Corvina, Budapest, 1979)

Mikes, George (Introduction) and Hamm, Manfred (Photographs), *Coffee Houses of Europe* (Thames and Hudson Ltd, London, 1980)

Monnier, Philippe, *Venice in the Eighteenth Century* (Chatto & Windus, London, 1910)

Peters, Catherine, *Thackeray: A Writer's Life* (Sutton Publishing, Stroud, Gloucestershire, 1999)

Powell, Jessica, *Literary Paris: A Guide* (The Little Bookroom, New York, 2006)

Rappaport, Helen, *Conspirator: Lenin in Exile* (Basic Books, New York, 2010)

Sayer, Derek, *Prague, Capital of the Twentieth Century: A Surrealist History* (Princeton University Press, Princeton, 2013)

Service, Robert, *Trotsky: A Biography* (Pan Macmillan, London, 2010)

Soria, Regina, *Elihu Vedder, American Visionary Artist in Rome 1836–1923* (Associated University Presses Inc., Cranbury, New Jersey, 1970)

Speer, Albert, *Inside the Third Reich* (The Macmillan Company, New York, 1970)

Török, András, *Budapest: A Critical Guide* (Pallas Athene, London, 1998)

Ukers, William H., *All About Coffee* (The Tea and Coffee Trade Journal Company, New York, 1922)

Wild, Anthony, *Black Gold* (Harper Perennial, London, 2005)

Newspapers, magazines, websites, blogs

Belén, Rodrigo, 'La magia del Café Gijón' (abc.es, 4 October 2015)

Bendová, Eva, 'The Lively World of Prague Coffee Houses' (The UK Friends of Czech Historic Buildings, Gardens and Parks newsletter, winter 2009/10)

Berry, Michael, 'Travesties' (sff.net, 28 May 2004)

Blanco, María José and Henn, David, 'Camilo José Cela: Censor, Novelist, Travel Writer and Editor' (periodistas-es.com, 13 May 2014)

Bulshtein, Ariel, 'A match made in Vienna: how coffeehouses shaped Jewish history' (*Israel Hayom*, 29 March 2022)

Burns, Tracy A., 'The artistic genius of Karel and Josef Čapek' (private-prague-guide.com, 2023)

Bush, Robert, 'Sitting With Sartre: Café de Flore' (medium.com, 4 August 2020)

Busk-Jepsen, Karen Benedicte, 'Caffè Greco: Art Temple, Post Office and Cosmopolitan Sanctuary' (The Thorvaldsens Museum Archives, 14 November 2022)

Chandler, Joseph, 'Philosophers' Paris' (*The Philosophers' Magazine*, 2023)

Cheng, Andrea, 'A historical look at Café de Flore' (crfashionbook.com, 11 July 2018)

Curtis, Stephanie, 'Bastille Day: Restaurants in France as Old as the Revolution' (*Los Angeles Times*, 14 July 1989)

De Boer, Sjoerd J., 'Hitler's Favourite Bars and Restaurants' (hitlerpages.com, 2006–2012)

De Frutos, Alberto, 'Aquí hay historia … El café Gijón' (*Historia de Iberia Vieja*, 22 July 2014)

Devane, Andy, 'Tracing the footsteps of Rome's foreign writers and artists' (*Wanted in Rome* magazine, October 2018)

Doolan, P.M., 'Café Odeon and Café Terrasse in Zürich' (doolanthinkshopblog.blogspot.com, 24 January 2010)

Duffy, Kathleen, 'A Short History of Oxford Coffee Houses and Student Life' (wizzley.com, 8 December 2013)

Esris, Elizabeth, 'James Baldwin: Scrutinizing America from Paris' (francerevisited.com, 12 October 2020)

Feiner, Muriel, 'The Café Gijón: the Spirit of Madrid since 1888' (guidepost.es, 28 November 2020)

Fleischhauer, Jan, 'Hitler's Underestimated Charisma' (*Spiegel International*, 11 October 2013)

Freedman, Ralph, 'Life of a Poet: Rainer Maria Rilke' (*The Washington Post*, 1996)

Gilpin, Eddy Kyle, 'Café Liberté: The Role of the Coffeehouse in the French Revolution' (*The Alexandrian* IX, no. 1, 2020)

Glynne-Jones, Jack, 'A social blend: the history of the Oxford coffeehouse' (cherwell.org, 6 June 2020)

Hanks, Eric, 'Why So Many African American Artists Moved to Paris in the 1920s' (pbs.org, 31 January 2022)

Hanson, Marilee, 'John Keats: Illness and Journey to Rome' (englishhistory.net, 22 February 2015)

Hay, Mark, 'In Istanbul Drinking Coffee In Public Was Once Punishable by Death' (atlasobscura.com, 22 May 2018)

Heath, David, 'Nazi-era Odeonsplatz, Nazi Sites on Munich's Ludwigstrasse and Munich's Adolf-Hitler-strasse and Schellingstrasse' (tracesofevil.com, 2023)

Hollway, Don, 'Fighter Pilot Hermann Göring' (scribd.com, 30 October 2018)

Jenkins, Stephanie, 'Oxford History: The High' (oxfordhistory.org.uk, 7 December 2022)

Johnson, Ben, 'English Coffeehouses, Penny Universities' (historic-uk.com, 2 May 2015)

Jones, Nigel, 'Love and Death in Vienna' (*The Critic*, 21 May 2020)

Kirsh, Andrea, 'The Forgotten Women Artists of Vienna 1900' (theartblog.org, 24 June 2012)

Kobbe, Montague, 'Camilo José Cela's The Hive Revisited' (3ammagazine.com, 22 January 2016)

Kollmeier, Kathrin, 'Thematic History Trail: National Socialism in Munich' (stadt.meunchen.de, 2010)

Kopsa, Andy, 'Czechoslovakia's Velvet Revolution Started 30 Years Ago – But It Was Decades in the Making' (*Time Magazine*, 16 November 2019)

Leadbeater, Chris, 'The Unheralded City that Put Coffee in Your Cup' (telegraph.co.uk, 23 January 2019)

Lockwood, Charles, 'In Search of the French Revolution in Paris' (*Chicago Tribune*, 29 January 1989)

Lozinska, Rita, 'Love story in paintings: Wassily Kandinsky and Gabriele Münter' (arthive.com, 21 October 2019)

Luke, Ben, 'Dada: 100 Years On' (*The Art Newspaper*, 1 March 2016)

Mambrol, Nasrulla, 'Analysis of Camilo José Cela's The Hive' (literariness.org, 12 October 2022)

Mandelkern, India, 'How to Make Seventeenth Century Coffee in Four Easy Steps' (huffpost.com, 6 December 2017)

Markham, James M., 'Goethe's Italian Journey' (*The New York Times*, 21 September 1986)

Marlowe, Lara, 'Centuries of stories lie behind Parisian café society' (*The Irish Times*, 7 July 2004)

Marquand, Robert, 'Café Serves as Witness to Cultural Slide' (*The Christian Science Monitor*, 19 June 1995)

Marshall, Colin, 'The Nazis' Philistine Grudge Against Abstract Art and the "Degenerate Art Exhibition" of 1937' (openculture.com, 7 November 2013)

McDonald, Michelle Craig, 'Coffeehouses' (*The Encyclopaedia of Greater Philadelphia*, 2016)

Nagy-Vargha, Zsófia, 'Then and Now: Legendary Sites of the Revolution of 1848' (*Hungary Today*, 15 March 2019)

Nelson, Fraser, '1711 and all that: the untold story of the Spectator' (spectator.co.uk, 1 March 2019)

Nicholson, Sarah, 'At Spanish cafes talk not time – is of the essence' (UPI Archives, 24 September 1985)

Ottiker, Marc, 'Meeting point in the grand café' (freitag.de, 7 January 2011)

Perrottet, Tony, 'Who Was Casanova?' (*Smithsonian Magazine*, April 2012)

Peters, Reed, 'History of Coffee Part 2: Spread of Coffee to Europe' (trulyexperiences.com, 25 March 2023)

Población, Félix, 'El Madrid Canalla del Café Gijón' (periodistas-es.com, 22 June 2014)

Ravvin, Norman, 'Singing at the Café Sztuka: Vera Gran's postwar trials' (*The Canadian Jewish News*, 13 January, 2015)

Rooney, Padraig, 'James Joyce in Zürich: Lust and Wanderlust' (*The Irish Times*, 24 November, 2015)

Rossi, Roberto, '"There will meet some learned gentlemen": Hogarth's Coffee House at St. John's Gate' (museumstjohn.org.uk, 5 November 2022)

Saunders, Beth, 'But First, Coffee: Caffè Greco and the Beginnings of Italian Photography' (metmuseum.org, 20 July 2017)

Sayer, Derek, 'Why I Love the Prague Coffee House Kafka Didn't Frequent' (zocalopublicsquare.org, 13 May 2014)

Taggart, Emma, 'Discover the Famous Works of Wassily Kandinsky, the Artist Who Painted Music' (mymodernmet.com, 13 December 2020)

Tamara, 'Coffee Houses in 17th Century England' (historynotes.info, 26 January 2014)

Tardi, Carla, 'Utilitarianism: What It Is, Founders, and Main Principles' (investopedia.com, 27 April 2023)

Thomas, Hugh, 'Seven Historic Places in London for Coffee Lovers' (timeout.com, 8 April 2016)

Thompson, Dave, 'Casanova and Voltaire' (casanovashadows.com, 2018)

Tomàs White, Cristina, 'La Generación Del 27: Spain's Tragic Literary Generation' (theculturetrip.com, 1 November 2016)

Trachtman, Paul, 'A Brief History of Dada' (*Smithsonian Magazine*, May 2006)

Tremlett, Giles, 'Spanish Novelist Spied for Franco's Regime' (*The Guardian*, 25 September 2004)

Tsaltas-Ottomanelli, 'The New York Tea Party' (Fraunces Tavern Museum, 2020)

Twardowski, Louise Ostermann, 'Sándor Petőfi: the building of a Hungarian legend' (kafkadesk.org, 20 November 2020)

Uziel, Daniel, '"Juden Unter Sich": The Propaganda Companies and the Jewish Ghettos in Occupied Poland' (visual-history.de, 20 April 2020)

Van Allen, Susan, 'Trieste: Italy's Surprising Capital of Coffee' (bbc.com, 19 January 2022)

Vargha, Dániel András, 'No Coffee, No Revolution?' (*Hungary Today*, 15 March 2022)

Voorhies, James, 'Surrealism' (metmuseum.org, October 2004)

Walker, Andy, '1913: When Hitler, Trotsky, Tito, Freud and Stalin all lived in the same place' (bbc.com, 20 March 2013)

Wipfler, Esther P., 'The Café Luitpold: coffee palace and artists' meeting place' (municharttogo, 2023)

Žantovský, Michael, 'Havel and Slavia' (Václav Havel Library Foundation, 2023)

Other sources

British Library European studies blog
Digital Encyclopaedia of European History
Encyclopaedia Britannica
encyclopedia.com
Free Library of Philadelphia
Imperial War Museum
Library of Congress
Massachusetts Historical Society
National Archives Museum, Washington DC
Paul Revere House
Poetry Foundation
Radio Free Europe and Radio Liberty
Radio Prague International
Warsaw Ghetto Museum
Washington Library, Mount Vernon
Wiener Holocaust Library
Wikipedia
YouTube

Index